I'm Not Supposed to Feel Like This

A Christian self-help approach to depression and anxiety

Chris Williams, Paul Richards and Ingrid Whitton

Hodder & Stoughton
LONDON SYDNEY AUCKLAND

First published in Great Britain in 2002

10 9 8 7 6 5 4 3 2 1

British Library Cataloguing in Publication Data
A record for this book is available from the British Library

ISBN 0 340 78639 6

Typeset by Avon Dataset Ltd, Bidford-on-Avon, Warks

Printed and bound in Great Britain by
The Guernsey Press Co. Ltd, Channel Isles

Hodder & Stoughton
A Division of Hodder Headline Ltd
338 Euston Road
London NW1 3BH

Contents

Foreword

The first time that I heard the phrase 'You can't be serious' I was a long way from the hallowed Centre Court at Wimbledon and indeed John McEnroe, in his now famous altercation with an umpire! I was coming towards the end of my higher studies at school, and had set my mind on reading psychology – or, to be more precise, 'Behavioural Science' – at university. The very idea that a committed Christian could contemplate such a course of study generated so strong a reaction among many of my friends that even I began to doubt whether I had made the right decision! Their reactions included:

> 'It's well known that psychology will disrupt your faith' . . . 'You can't believe in God and use all those therapies' . . . 'Psychology? – You can't be serious; you will leave university as an atheist!'

Four years later, I graduated with an honours degree in Behavioural Science – but perhaps even more important, I emerged as a much stronger Christian. People do panic when it comes to issues of the mind!

Having been through the discipline of thinking through challenges to faith, and having faced up to understanding the correlation between belief and behaviour, I now find myself increasingly excited with the opportunity to affirm the place of psychology and psychiatric methodology in the holistic development of self-awareness and self-help. Hence my delight in having been asked to write the foreword to this book.

The science of the mind has not always enjoyed good press, but most of the negativism has emerged from unwise practice, and more specifically, practitioners who have hijacked good principles and made them into bad practice. Many Christian people have subsequently beileved the headline without understanding the story!

How refreshing therefore to see this publication in our bookstores – firmly grounded in Scripture, but committed to a sound, psychological approach – good, wholesome and, what's more, wonderfully effective. To understand how the mind works and how thought processes impinge upon our behaviour patterns initially requires a great degree of honesty. Self-reflection is all part of personal growth, and honesty is always rewarded with healthy development.

Depression and anxiety are experienced by many Christians in the pressure cooker of life. Recognising and accepting that worry, feelings of inadequacy, guilt and even despair are 'allowed' is a major leap forward for those who have been convinced that this is all part of 'Cross-carrying' pain! Even more concerning is the suggestion that these feelings are basically satanic. The devil often gets blamed for more than he deserves!

Of course spiritual warfare is real, but an added blessing in this book is the healthy balance between the spiritual and the mental. Those who feel desperately ill with worry and depression have, for too long, been encouraged to simply 'pull themselves together' or have been given some spiritual platitude plucked fresh from the pages of the New Testament. When you are ill, even well meaning advice can fall on deaf ears and at times becomes unhelpful.

With its constant encouragement to apply a healthy degree of self-enquiry and examination, a troubled reader will find great help and support on these pages. There is a wealth of practical advice to help those who need sustained medical attention, and church leaders, often at a loss to cope with hurting people, will find here a treasury of good pastoral resources.

It was the French Philosopher Descartes who said, '*Cogito ergo sum* – I think, therefore I am' – a phrase that takes us to the rationale of cognitive behaviour therapy and indeed the thrust of this book. In the mêlée of socialisation, peer group pressure, the influences of important figures in our lives and a whole host of other experiences, thought processes emerge which can have a helpful or unhelpful impact on how we see ourselves and other people.

I hope that this book will be more than 'a good read'. To understand the implications will necessitate some active thought, meditation and prayer. And for those of you thinking that God has let you or others down, or are too tired to pray, there are words that will help guide you through the recovery process.

God grants us permission to own up to feeling unwell, but also gives us the means to get better! This book is a timely addition to the dispensary, and can be an important resource on the journey to recovery.

Dave Pope
January 2002

Introduction
and how to use this book

Depression and anxiety are common difficulties both in general society and also within the Church. Psychiatric problems can create particular issues for Christians. Studies in the USA show that over 60 per cent of people with depression blame themselves and see sin as a contributing cause. Many Christians and some church workers incorrectly believe that we 'shouldn't' get depressed and that psychiatric problems are the result of a poor or damaged relationship with God.

This book is written for Christians who find that they are feeling depressed and/or anxious, and also for their fellow church members and church workers so that they can offer more effective and helpful support. We hope that it will provide a useful resource for clergy and lay leaders, pastoral and ministry team members and Christian counselling and support teams.

We believe that insights from both the psychiatric profession and the Bible have much to teach about worry, fear and depression and that both provide valuable resources for those experiencing these common problems.

This book uses a self-help approach and encourages the reader to find out for themselves about the causes and treatment of their own depression and anxiety. It is clearly structured, with a print size and layout that makes it both accessible and easy to use. Throughout the book we have used examples from the Bible and 'real life' to illustrate common difficulties that people face. These are based upon our own experience of working to help others. However, we have made sure that no examples reflect anyone known to us directly. We also discuss step-by-step approaches to overcome these problems. The approach is based upon the principles of Cognitive Behaviour Therapy (CBT) – a proven and effective treatment that is fully compatible with the Christian faith. In addition, suggestions for focused prayer and meditations from the Bible will provide you with a clear plan of things you can do to improve how you feel.

THE STRUCTURE OF THE BOOK

The book is split into four parts. *Part 1* will help you begin to think about the unity of God's design for us. He has created us with an ability to think and react to the different situations, relationships and practical problems that we all face in everyday life.

In *Part 2* of the book you will discover how depression and anxiety act to distort not only how we see and think about ourselves, but also our view of those around us and our attitudes towards the different events that we face in life. Depression and anxiety worsen any in-built tendency to see ourselves as 'bad' or as 'failures' and may cause us to focus on the negative in things in an unhelpful and unbalanced way. These extreme and unhelpful ways of seeing things can worsen how we feel, and unhelpfully alter what we do. They can worsen our relationship with others and with God. This part of the book will help you discover the impact on you of such thinking, and help you understand its origins.

The chapters in *Part 3* will help you to learn new ways of overcoming feelings of anxiety and depression. This builds upon the reader's faith and relationship with God and looks at how this can be maintained and developed during times of distress; it encourages an approach to recovery that includes prayer, reading the Bible, gaining helpful support from others and putting into practice a range of actions to help identify and change unhelpful thinking styles and activities that might be worsening how you feel. We will also take a closer look at our relationship with our church fellowship; how it can be a source of encouragement and support and assist the healing process.

Finally, in *Part 4* the last chapter contains helpful information for clergy and lay leadership about how the local church can play a significant part in the process of recovery from anxiety and depression.

USING THIS BOOK

The content is designed so that you can easily dip in to certain chapters if they cover particular problem areas you have. *You might find it most helpful to read Parts 1 and 2 first* as these will help you to understand the causes and impact of your problems. The chapters in Part 3 will then help you to discover what to do to begin to overcome those problems. As you read the book, it is important to be realistic in your expectations of how quickly you will improve. Recovery from anxiety and depression may take a number of months, and patience is an important part of recovery. We hope that this book, together with other treatments from your doctor or health care practitioner, will help you on the way, and also encourage you spiritually.

As you read each chapter, try to really think about what you are reading and, in particular, consider how what you are reading might apply to you. To help you do this, each chapter is divided into clear sections. If you are feeling depressed, you may have noticed that your energy and concentration levels are not as good as they would normally have been. If this is true for you, bear this in mind when reading the book. You may find it easier to set yourself the goal of *reading just one section of a chapter at a time* – try to be realistic as to how much you read at once. Similarly if you think there is too much to take in at once, it is a good idea to try to read each chapter quite slowly to allow yourself thinking time so that you can get as much out of it as possible.

As you read each section:

- You will find mention of *specific Bible passages*. These use examples from the Bible that illustrate important principles for understanding anxiety and depression, God's relationship with us, and about helpful responses that we can make to recover. They also remind us of God's promises to us of forgiveness, and of his faithfulness towards us. From time to time we will also ask you to *reflect and pray* about certain passages, to consider what God can teach you now. Unless indicated otherwise, passages that are quoted are taken from the New International Version (NIV) of the Bible.
- Try to answer all the questions asked. The process of having to *stop, think and reflect* on how the questions might be relevant to you is a crucial part of getting better.
- You will probably find that some aspects of each chapter are more useful to you at the moment than others. That is normal – just try to focus on the helpful bits that apply to you. Write down your own notes of key points in the margins or in the '*My notes*' area at the end of the chapter to help you remember information that has been helpful. Plan to review your notes regularly to help you apply what you have learned.
- Once you have read through an entire chapter, some readers may find it helpful to put it on one side and then reread it a few days later. It may be that different parts of it become clearer, or seem more useful, on second reading.
- Within each chapter, important areas are labelled as '*key points*'. Certain areas that are covered may not be relevant for everyone. Such areas will be clearly identified so that you can choose to skip optional material if you wish.
- Throughout the book, 'real life' examples are provided to help

build understanding. All examples have been created for this book.

- Think about discussing what you learn with a few trusted people such as Christian friends, church leaders or your health care practitioner. If you would prefer them not to mention your conversation to others, ask them to agree to this and choose these people carefully so that you talk to those whose confidentiality you trust.

CREDITS

We wish to thank Revd Phil Malloch and Mr Stuart McChlery who have commented upon selected content of this book. We also would like to thank Alison, Lynne and Phil who have offered suggestions, help and support during the writing of this book.

Each of the authors is a committed Christian with a wish to help believers suffering from anxiety or depression towards healing. Our hope and prayer is that this book will be helpful to you in that process.

Chris Williams, Paul Richards, Ingrid Whitton
March 2002

PART 1: A CHRISTIAN VIEW ON ANXIETY AND DEPRESSION

1

What I think affects how I feel and what I do

This book is written for Christians who have found that they themselves or those they know are experiencing problems of anxiety and/or depression. Our key goal is to help readers understand more about anxiety and depression and learn how to tackle these problems in ways that build upon their own Christian faith.

Our approach

The authors are all committed Christians and the book is written from a Christian standpoint. We believe that a person's relationship with God can be important in helping them overcome problems such as anxiety and depression. If you are not a Christian, or are sceptical about the Christian faith, then this book will contain material that may seem strange to you. This includes an emphasis on learning from the Bible and also the suggestion that there is a role for prayer in addition to other practical approaches that can be useful in improving how you feel. You will find out exactly what we mean by the terms 'anxiety' and 'depression' in Chapter 2. If you are not a Christian, hopefully you will be able to get some useful hints and tips for how to approach these problems, and you may also find that the spiritual aspects of the book are interesting and at times helpful.

- *What we believe*: We believe that all Christians can experience worry, fear, upset and depression. We also believe that being a Christian does not prevent us or our loved ones from experiencing upsetting and challenging problems such as illness, unemployment, or relationship and other practical difficulties. Sometimes these problems can reach such a level and last for such a long time that they cause significant upset for us and also to those around us.
- *What we do not believe*: Although at times we all choose to act in ways that are wrong and this can lead to bad consequences for us and for others, we do not see anxiety and depression as always being the result of sin; neither do we believe that mental health problems are the result of a lack of faith.

Key point: Part of anxiety and depression is a tendency to judge things in extreme and unhelpful ways that distort how we see ourselves, God, people we know and the events that occur to us. These extreme ways of seeing things are often learned very early on in our lives and such unhelpful thinking tends to worsen when we feel anxious or depressed. Unhelpful thinking often becomes worse when we face difficult situations, relationship or practical problems, particularly when we think that we are trapped and overwhelmed.

Part of the answer to overcoming these unhelpful ways of seeing things is to look again at how God sees us. So we start now with a discussion of God's plan for how we should live. Later on we will consider the impact of our being brought up within a damaged and damaging world. Finally, towards the end of this chapter we will think about the implications for us as Christians as we try to change our old unhelpful patterns of thinking after we become believers.

SECTION 1: IN THE BEGINNING . . .

God's design for each of us

God has created each of us to be unique. We each look, sound, think and act very differently from everyone else. We have our own hopes and fears, strengths and weaknesses. Each person's uniqueness is planned by God – and the fact that he can bring such different people together within the unity of the Church is a miracle in itself. The result is that our individual differences add to the strength and diversity of the Church.

What does the Bible say?
Read 1 Corinthians 12:12–13:13.
What does this say about our uniqueness and role?

Science tries to explain some of these differences through the study of how people think – psychology. This can helpfully cast some light onto our understanding of God's design of us as human beings. One important development in psychology is the Cognitive (meaning 'thinking') Behaviour Therapy (CBT) approach, and this book seeks to use insights from CBT in combination with biblical principles to help understand and plan ways of overcoming problems of anxiety and depression. Central to this approach are our *beliefs/thoughts*. The CBT approach suggests that what we think/believe affects how we feel emotionally and physically, and also what we do.

Links occur between each of these areas – thinking, our emotio[illegible] and physical feelings, and our behaviour.

Illustration: This idea can be illustrated by recalling how you felt the last time you had a severe cold, flu or a virus. How did you feel mentally? Were you alert, able to concentrate with a good attention span? In all probability you felt mentally unfocused and below par, and your mood was lowered by the viruses your body was fighting. Most of us expect this, yet we often do not expect our spiritual life to be any different from normal when our bodies and minds are affected in anxiety or depression.

It is a simple fact that if we are experiencing depression or anxiety, our spiritual life is likely to be affected too. Prayer may be a constant struggle and worship may require of us an energy we simply do not possess. Attempts to read the Bible may flounder after a few short minutes as our attention wanders from one thing to another. In such a situation it is easy to feel cut off from God – angry with him for deserting us, or angry with ourselves for not being able to break through to a sense of God's presence. One thing that can help us a great deal when we feel depressed is to recognise the likelihood of our feelings about God fluctuating, along with our feelings about everything else.

nal

ɹences of the 'Fall'

how God first designed us to live.

Task: Read Genesis 2:15–25.

Q. What was the man's and the woman's relationship with God like when they were first created?

Q. What was their relationship with each other like?

Genesis 3 goes on to describe how through choice mankind sinned and damaged previously close relationships with God, with fellow human beings and with the environment. The consequences of this are that we now live in a world where life can be painful and difficult. We see this in the moral, ethical, physical, economic and spiritual problems that occur around us and that sometimes result in damage and suffering to us and those we care about.

Our unhelpful thinking styles

One consequence of the Fall is that we are brought up in a world that has been damaged, and our own experience of being brought up is likely to have damaged us in at least some ways. No matter how loving our parents have been, they will not always have reacted in the ways that we really needed. For some of us, our experience with our parents will have been largely a good one, for others it may have been very bad. Whatever your own experiences, it is likely that as you grew up you learned a range of *helpful and unhelpful rules* about how you see and judge yourself, other people and the world around you. It is in childhood that these central ways of seeing things are first learned from your relationship with important people such as parent or parents, brothers or sisters. In these relationships you should have received love, consistency and support, but sometimes the opposite occurs – rejection and inconsistency – and this can undermine us as we grow up. These central ways of seeing things are called *core beliefs.*

Common core beliefs may be based around positive themes such as seeing yourself as good or successful at something, or more negative themes such as being a failure, bad, worthless, unlovable, incompetent, foolish or weak. Most people develop a range of both positive and negative core beliefs during their childhood and these can stay with us into our adult lives. Most of the time when the more negative core beliefs come to mind, we can dismiss them; however, during times of distress, anxiety and depression, not only are people more prone to notice their negative core beliefs, but also such thoughts occur more frequently.

Q. At times when you feel distressed, do you recognise any of these sorts of thoughts in yourself?

1. Attitudes about how you see yourself

I am totally:

Bad	Yes ❑	No ❑
Unlovable	Yes ❑	No ❑
Worthless/unworthy	Yes ❑	No ❑
Incompetent/stupid	Yes ❑	No ❑
Powerless/weak	Yes ❑	No ❑
A failure	Yes ❑	No ❑

2. Attitudes about how you see others

Others are always:

Untrustworthy	Yes ❑	No ❑
Manipulative	Yes ❑	No ❑
Letting me down	Yes ❑	No ❑
Better than me	Yes ❑	No ❑

These sorts of beliefs can cause us problems when we become Christians. For example, someone who has had experiences of being let down by others may have fears that God or the Church will let them down. Someone who has had a parent who does not show them very much love may find it difficult accepting that God can really love them. Likewise, someone who has had experiences of a distant, unloving or manipulative human father may well have problems identifying with the idea that God can be a trustworthy and loving Father.

These sorts of thoughts are very common and normal experiences, but they are unhelpful. They are also untrue, and really just rules that we have learned as a result of growing up in a fallen world. *They are not from God. God never judges his followers as* ***total*** *failures or* ***totally*** *damaged or worthless.* He cares for us unconditionally and, while recognising our faults, he looks at us in love and sees 'Christ is in us'.

God washes us from our sins and forgives us. Even when we *feel* totally guilty or worthless, he does not judge us like that. He does not make global, all-or-nothing judgments of our failure; instead he convicts us of *specific* things that we need to change, so that we can move on in relationship with him. In the process of moving forward he will be there to uphold us (Jeremiah 31:3–4, 25). We need to recognise our negative core beliefs for what they are because, in spite of them being false, they can nevertheless become self-fulfilling prophecies. Even when we fail, the wonderful thing about God is that his final word to us is always grace and never condemnation.

What does the Bible say?

- We are no longer condemned by God: 'There is now no condemnation for those who are in Christ Jesus' (Romans 8:1).
- God loves us unconditionally: 'This is how God showed his love among us: He sent his one and only Son into the world that we might live through him. This is love: not that we loved God, but that he loved us and sent his Son as an atoning sacrifice for our sins' (1 John 4:9–10).
- God forgives us: 'If we confess our sins, he is faithful and just and will forgive us our sins and purify us from all unrighteousness' (1 John 1:9).

When we are Christians, if we have thoughts that we are *totally* bad/worthless/failed, etc. this condemnation *never* comes from God. You can begin to challenge these untrue and unhelpful thinking styles by noticing these thoughts, and countering them with the promises of God in the Bible.

Sometimes when depression is at a high level it may seem that nothing can make any difference and it may feel impossible to make any changes. If this is the case, try to just read small parts of the book – perhaps just a single page – and we suggest moving to Part 3 of the book, which will provide you with some more immediate suggestions of things you can do to help move forwards. If you are feeling like this, it is also important to discuss this with your health care practitioner.

SECTION 3

God's divine rescue plan

We have read the account of how God created man and woman to be in a correct relationship with him and with each other earlier in this chapter. This correct relationship was then broken, and what follows in the Old and New Testaments is the account of how God has set about restoring that relationship until it reaches perfection. His eventual goal for us as Christians is to have a perfect relationship with him and each other again. This relationship is seen at the very start of the Bible (in Genesis) and the end of the Bible (in Revelation). As Christians we are each constantly going through the process of building this relationship with him.

The Christian pathway

We are each travelling down the Christian path and this path will include both ups and downs. God is with you wherever you are on this path, and can work things out for the good, no matter how difficult they seem at the moment. Part of Christian maturity is to be able to begin to see yourself as God sees you – as someone who is loved by him in spite of the areas we all have in our lives that continue to be wrong. We have his promise that he will continue to work in us and change us so that we increasingly reflect his own character (2 Corinthians 3:18). We can depend upon this promise because God is completely and always trustworthy.

The process of being a Christian is often an ongoing challenge to us as people – we want to be in the right relationship with God and with his community in the Church, but constantly fall short of the mark – in short, we sin. The problem is that God has called us to think, feel and act in ways that all of us as Christians have difficulty with. He calls us to love when at times we feel hatred, he calls us to peace when at times we are scared, he calls us to follow when at times we wish to be disobedient.

Task: Read the following passage and compare this with your own experience of life as a Christian:

Romans 7:14–8:5 – Paul's inner battles. Paul wanted to change but continued to be tempted. He recognised that he could succeed only through Jesus.

Write down the key struggles that Paul had.

Do you notice any of the same struggles in your own life?

How you make this judgment may be affected by what you think about yourself and your relationship with God, and how close you feel to God. You may find it is also affected by how you feel physically and how many life difficulties you are currently facing. At times when you are distressed, it is quite possible that you will rate yourself more critically than God or your fellow Christians would.

You will find out a lot more about how each of these areas may affect your faith and your relationship with God in Part 2 of the book.

Key point: Sometimes we judge ourselves more harshly than God judges us. One problem with our old unhelpful thinking styles and core beliefs is that we can sometimes believe that they are true even when God tells us that they are not.

For example:

- He tells us he loves us and we have *great* value to him – when sometimes we see ourselves as totally worthless.
- As Christians, he sees us as good, blameless and washed from sin – whereas we may sometimes see ourselves as wholly bad and guilty.
- He tells us that as Christians we will eventually be victorious – when sometimes we judge ourselves as only being failures. Ignoring our victories and the positive things he does in us, we may unhelpfully tend to focus only on our defeats.

You will find out more about this in Parts 2 and 3 of the book and start to discover ways that allow you to see God's true view of you rather than your own often distorted one.

If you think like this at all, use the Bible verses at the end of this chapter to help you to begin to challenge these thoughts. Remember they are God's promises and can be trusted.

The good news is that God does not leave us alone in this battle. He promises:

- That he loves us: he never judges us as bad or worthless. He loves and accepts us in spite of our sin. He forgives us because of what Jesus did.

  When you were dead in your sins and in the uncircumcision of your sinful nature, God made you alive with Christ. He forgave us all our sins, having cancelled the written code, with its regulations, that was against us and that stood opposed to us; he took it away, nailing it to the cross. And having disarmed the powers and authorities, he made a public spectacle of them, triumphing over them by the cross (Colossians 2:13–15).

- He will never let us go and will always love us. 'For I am convinced that neither death nor life, neither angels nor demons, neither the present nor the future, nor any powers, neither height nor depth, nor anything in all creation, will be able to separate us from the love of God that is in Christ Jesus our Lord' (Romans 8:38–9).

- The indwelling help of the Holy Spirit, who acts as a teacher and encourager (John 14:25–7; 16:5–15) and pleads on our behalf to God. 'In the same way, the Spirit helps us in our weakness. We do not know what to pray for, but the Spirit himself intercedes for us with groans that words cannot express. And he who searches our hearts knows the mind of the Spirit because the Spirit intercedes for the saints in accordance with God's will' (Romans 8:26–7).

- The prayers of Jesus on our behalf and the support of others in the Church to help us along the way. 'Therefore he is able to save completely those who come to God through him, because he always lives to intercede for them' (Hebrews 7:25).

Important point

Every Christian has times of doubt, fear and failure – and also times when they feel distant from God. These feelings are a normal part of the Christian walk. When we are feeling distressed, doubt often grows and we become overly self-critical. It is important to remember that we all fail to live life as God wants us to. *That's why Jesus came to save us!* We are all sinners, but sinners whom God is changing. God changes us at his own pace – at times quite rapidly, but frequently quite slowly. He renews our minds and changes our attitudes so that we increasingly have the mind of Christ (1 Corinthians 2:16).

He promises that no matter what happens to us, he will work for good in us (Romans 8:28). Even when we are anxious or depressed, he will help us through this, and use what has happened to help us to grow as Christians. We hope that this book will help you in this process.

Summary

In this chapter you have learned about:

- God's design for us.
- How the Fall has damaged our relationship with God and each other and this has resulted in us learning unhelpful thinking styles in how we see ourselves, God and others.
- God's divine rescue plan is to change these attitudes so that we love God and others.
- The Christian life can be difficult, but God sticks with us, and promises that he will work for the good in us no matter what.
- Our Christian attitudes lead us to alter what we do. He wants us to move away from problem attitudes and instead live lives as he wants us to – seeing and judging things as he does.

Putting into practice what you have learned

You will get the most out of what you have learned if you can put it into action this week. Pray the following prayer, then read and reflect on the Bible verses that follow over the next week or so.

CLOSING PRAYER

When you can, pray this prayer silently or preferably aloud.

Father God, thank you that you chose to make me the person that I am. Thank you for the gift of Jesus to restore my relationship with you. Even though some parts of my life are a struggle at the moment I want to tell you that I trust you and believe that you have plans for my wellbeing. Please help me as I seek to understand more about myself and grow through this difficult period of my life. As I begin to read this book, please help me to remember and put into practice those things that you want me to learn.

I also think of others reading this book and pray that they will also find benefit.

Amen.

Bible meditation

Find somewhere quiet and then slowly read the verses that follow. Ask God what he is trying to tell you. Reflect and pray on how this is relevant to you. Remind yourself of what the Bible says and focus on this when you notice any old negative beliefs:

- We are no longer condemned by God: 'There is no condemnation for those who are in Christ Jesus' (Romans 8:1).
- God loves us unconditionally: 'This is how God showed his love among us: He sent his one and only Son into the world that we might live through him. This is love: not that we loved God, but

that he loved us and sent his Son as an atoning sacrifice for our sins' (1 John 4:9–10).

- God forgives us: 'If we confess our sins, he is faithful and just and will forgive us our sins and purify us from all unrighteousness' (1 John 1:9).

Write these verses out and carry them around with you so that you can remind yourself of their truth when you need to.

> **Key point:** When we are Christians, if we have thoughts that we are totally bad/worthless/failures, etc., this condemnation *never* comes from God.

My notes

PART 2:

UNDERSTANDING ANXIETY AND DEPRESSION

2

What anxiety and depression are and how they affect us

In this chapter you will find out what is meant by the terms 'anxiety' and 'depression', then look at how they can affect our thoughts, bodies, emotions and behaviour using the Five Areas Model. You will then have the chance to complete your own Five Areas Assessment, and finally to look at the Cognitive Behaviour Therapy (CBT) approach to treatment. Throughout we will be looking at these issues from a Christian point of view, and examining how anxiety and depression affect you in your relationship with God, with other people and with your church.

Definitions

We wish to start this section with a clear definition of what we mean by the terms 'depression', 'anxiety' and the very high levels of sudden-onset anxiety known as 'panic'. Together, these affect more than one in five people at some time in their lives.

What is depression?

Feeling fed up and low in mood is a normal part of life. When difficulties or upsetting events occur it is not unusual to feel down, stop enjoying things and to feel low for a time as a reaction to events. Likewise when good things happen, a person may experience happiness, pleasure and a sense of achievement. The reasons for low mood are usually clear – a stressful situation, a relationship difficulty, feeling let down by someone, financial difficulties, unforeseen events or some other practical problem. Most of the time the drop in mood only lasts for a short period of time and then we 'bounce back'.

Occasionally, however, a person's mood may seem to fall for little or no obvious reason and it may be difficult to begin with to know quite why. In some cases this 'depressed' feeling can worsen and completely dominate the person's life. When someone feels very low for more than two weeks and feels like this day after day, week after week, this is called a '*depressive illness*'. It is important to say that there should be no stigma attached to the diagnosis of 'depression'. In reality the term is simply a convenient way of describing a broad range of symptoms that vary from person to person but are having an unhelpful impact on their lives.

What is anxiety?

Anxiety, worry, tension and stress are all terms that are used to describe what is a widespread experience for many people. Anxiety is a common emotion, which at times can be helpful even though it can feel very unpleasant. For example, in situations of danger we begin to feel anxious and this prompts us to try to deal with the threatening situation by getting away from it as rapidly as possible. If you walk along a badly maintained path next to a large drop, anxiety can be life-saving, appropriate and helpful. However, sometimes anxiety can occur inappropriately and then it becomes unhelpful. The person may feel anxious in situations that are not really dangerous at all, or notice excessive anxiety well beyond what is actually helpful or appropriate in the circumstances.

Worrying thoughts are common in anxiety. In worry, the person goes over things again and again in their mind in a way that is unhelpful because it does not actually help to resolve the difficulty that is being worried about. Instead, problems are turned over and thought about again and again. Sometimes the worry may be out of all proportion; something that may originally have happened in a few moments, perhaps something that someone has said to you, can dominate your thinking for much of the following days or weeks, adding up in total to many days or even weeks of worry over the following months.

In anxiety, the person often *overestimates* the threat or danger they are facing, and at the same time usually *underestimates* their own capacity to cope with the problem.

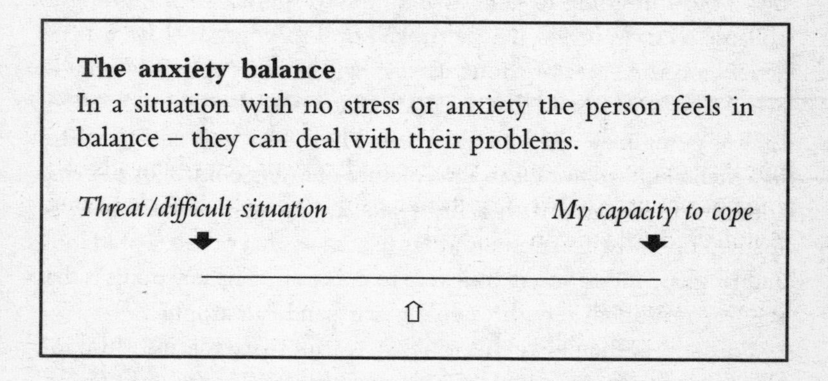

Normally, when there is no stress, the person feels *able to cope* with the problems they face. In other situations, they may begin to feel stressed. Either they see the problem as too large or overwhelming, or they think they cannot cope. In both situations, the anxiety balance is upset, and the person begins to feel increasingly stressed and upset. At times of emotional distress, it is sometimes easy to forget that we are not alone when we face life's difficulties – we have not only our own capacity to cope but also the support and love God offers us.

What are panic attacks?

Sometimes anxiety can come on very rapidly (usually within ten minutes) to such a high level that the person feels so mentally and physically tense and unwell that they stop what they are doing and try to leave or escape from the situation. Failing that, they may become paralysed into inactivity – like rabbits caught in the headlamps of a car – and just wait, expecting disaster to strike at any moment. They do this because they fear that something terrible or catastrophic will happen. This feeling of acute fear, dread or terror is called a 'panic attack'. Panic attacks typically have a rapid onset and are short-lived, usually lasting no longer than twenty to thirty minutes.

During panic, the person can experience catastrophic fears that a sudden and threatening physical illness or terrible event will occur *right now*. 'I'm going to faint', 'I'm going to suffocate', 'I'm going to collapse', 'I'm going to have a stroke', or 'I'm going to have a heart attack' are the sorts of thoughts that will go through their minds. Sometimes the fear is that a catastrophic mental event will occur, such as going mad and losing control. These fears may take the form of a mental image (for example, a picture of losing control or of being admitted to hospital with a heart attack). Sometimes fears may be focused upon the reaction of others (e.g. a fear that others would look and laugh or mock you if you were to collapse). The key point is that the fear is immediately threatening, scary and catastrophic.

Sometimes the person becomes so fearful that even just thinking about the situations and places where panics have previously occurred may result in them feeling anxious. They may find themselves worrying that a further panic attack will occur and this anticipation itself can add to the person's anxiety. The person commonly reacts by avoiding anything to do with that situation or place. The result is often an increasingly restricted lifestyle, reduced confidence and additional long-term distress. When this happens, the person is described as having a *phobia* as well as panic attacks. A phobia is anxiety that regularly occurs in a specific situation.

You may have heard of people who have panic attacks on buses or in shops or crowded situations – the most common form of phobia, which is sometimes called 'agoraphobia'. Panic attacks also commonly occur in other specific situations (in open spaces, and in phobias of certain animals such as spiders and snakes, and even such apparently harmless creatures as butterflies). In some cases the person may not have a specific fear or anxiety but experience panic attacks when other upsets or fears build up and up in their minds.

It is important to realise that problems of anxiety, depression and panic may occur together, or quite separately. However they are affecting you, this chapter will help you to find out more about the causes of these, and help you to begin to plan ways of changing this.

How common are depression, anxiety and panic?

Depression and anxiety are far more common experiences than most people think. Anxiety and depression can affect anyone. Some well-known people have suffered from them. You may have seen television programmes or read books about their experience of tackling these problems. Around one in five people experience depression and at least one in ten people experience a panic attack at some time in their lives. It is extremely likely that you will know one or two friends, family members or people at church who regularly experience these problems, and there will probably be many more Christians in your church who are suffering from depression, anxiety and panic than you are aware of because of the unwillingness of many believers to admit to having such experiences.

Being a Christian does not prevent difficulties arising in our lives

The title of this book, *I'm Not Supposed to Feel Like This*, has been chosen partly because that is exactly how many of us react to finding that we are depressed or anxious. One of the main reasons for writing this book is to help those with such difficulties – first to say that you are not unusual and second that you are not alone.

Being a Christian does not inoculate us from the possibility of experiencing anxiety or depression; several Christian psychiatrists have experienced quite severe depressive illnesses, and if it can happen to them it can certainly happen to the rest of us. This is true in the same way that being a Christian does not prevent you from becoming ill or falling victim to crime or assault.

For example:

- Paul was imprisoned (Acts 16:23).
- Paul was shipwrecked (Acts 27:27–44).
- Jesus himself – ridiculed, beaten and killed (Matthew 21:11–50).
- David was threatened by Saul (1 Samuel 19:1).

These practical difficulties are the sort of problems that may lead to emotional difficulties such as anxiety and depression.

It is worth remembering that the apostle Paul, who wrote confidently of all things working together for good for those who love God (Romans 8:28), also described his experiences in the following terms:

> I have . . . been in prison more frequently, been flogged more severely, and been exposed to death again and again. Five times I received from the Jews the forty lashes minus one. Three times I was beaten with rods, once I was stoned, three times I was shipwrecked, I spent a night and a day in the open sea . . . I have been in danger from rivers, in danger from bandits, in danger from my own countrymen, in danger from Gentiles; in danger in the city, in danger in the country, in danger at sea . . . I have laboured and toiled and have often gone without sleep; I have known hunger and thirst and have often gone without food; I have been cold and naked (2 Corinthians 11:23–7).

Paul still believed that God was able to work for good even in these circumstances, but it would be foolish to pretend his life was easy. Generally speaking, while God protects us and holds our lives in his hands, he also allows us to experience the consequences of living in a world that has rebelled against his laws and knows pain, distress and corruption. We may be protected through tough times, and even the most severe difficulties may serve God's purpose in the long run, but there is little in the Bible to support the idea that unpleasant experiences should not come our way. The purpose of our faith is to encourage us that God is, ultimately, in control, and even the most difficult of our experiences can be opportunities for growth, both for ourselves and his kingdom.

Exercise

Think about the following people in the Bible who have experienced feelings of being low or anxious/worried. Allow yourself a few minutes to reflect on the problems faced by these Bible characters.

Example 1

Joseph in:

- Genesis 37:17–28.
- Genesis 39:6–21.
- Genesis 50:18–23.

Example 2

Naomi in:

- Ruth 1.

Key point: The fact that God's people, even some of his greatest servants, can experience deep distress and feelings of anxiety or depression is important. This reminds us of three very important truths:

- That we as Christians may become anxious or depressed.
- That God continues to love us and stay with us in spite of how we feel.
- We are not failures or inadequate Christians because we experience such things.

Remember

- What Moses said to the Israelites facing the uncertainty of the promised land and the might of foreign armies can apply equally to us when we face such difficulties: 'Be strong and courageous. Do not be afraid or terrified because of them, for the LORD your God goes with you; he will never leave you nor forsake you' (Deuteronomy 31:6).
- 'I am he, I am he who will sustain you. I have made you and I will carry you; I will sustain you and I will rescue you' (Isaiah 46:4).
- 'The righteous cry out and the LORD hears them; he delivers them from their troubles. The LORD is close to the broken-hearted and saves those who are crushed in spirit' (Psalm 34:17–18).

A key component of our reaction as Christians to problems in life is prayer and turning to God at times when things are really difficult (Psalm 130:1). Our faith can be a major source of support to us when facing difficult situations, and you will find out more about how to act most effectively to help overcome distress in Part 3 of this book.

In the next section of this chapter we want to focus on understanding the ways in which anxiety and depression affect us as people, because understanding these things will help us to use biblical values to overcome our difficulties.

What you need to know to understand anxiety and depression

In this section we want to introduce you to one of the most important tools we use in this book, called 'The Five Areas of Anxiety and Depression'. You might find that it takes a little time to understand and get to grips with this idea, but it will be well worth it when you have understood the principles we are speaking about.

When anxiety or depression occur, they affect the person's mood and thinking, they lead to altered behaviour and interfere with daily activities and they create a range of unpleasant physical symptoms in the body. Each of these changes can then act, alone or together, to keep the anxiety or depression going. The word 'altered' is used because in anxiety and depression, changes occur in each of these important aspects of our lives so that we think, feel and act in ways that are different from usual.

The Five Areas we are speaking of, that are linked together, are:

1. Life situation (relationships, practical problems and difficulties).
2. Altered thinking.
3. Altered feelings (also called 'moods' or 'emotions').
4. Altered physical feelings/bodily symptoms.
5. Altered behaviour or activity levels.

Key point: The diagram on page 38 captioned 'The Five Areas of Anxiety and Depression' shows that what a person *thinks* about a situation or problem may affect how they *feel physically and emotionally*, and also alters what they *do* (behaviour or activity). Each of these five areas (situation, relationship or practical problems, thinking, emotional and physical feelings, and behaviour changes) affects all the other areas.

A Five Areas Assessment can help you begin to understand the links between each of these areas in your own life. Think about the examples that follow the diagram:

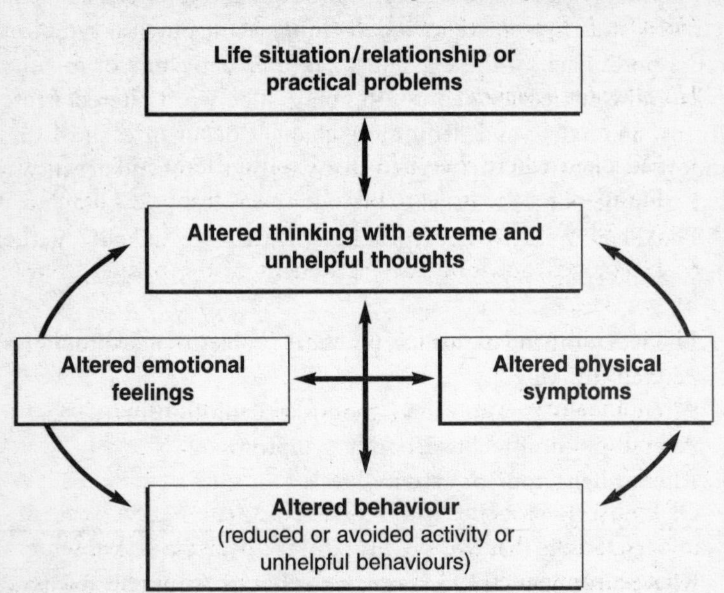

Example 1: Jesus and the death of Lazarus

John 11:1–44 tells the story of the death and raising from the dead of Lazarus. Looking at the events that occurred in detail:

Situation: Mary (the sister of Lazarus) fell at the feet of Jesus and said 'Lord, if you had been here, my brother would not have died' (v. 32).

His altered thinking: Jesus had compassion for them (v. 33). His thoughts focused on meeting the needs of the upset relatives and friends, and on asking his Father for the miracle, 'that they may believe that you sent me' (v. 42).

His altered emotional feelings: He was deeply moved (v. 38) and troubled (v. 33).

His altered physical feelings: He wept (v. 35).

His altered behaviour:

- He asked where they had laid Lazarus' body (v. 34).
- He asked for the stone to be rolled away from the entrance (vv. 38–9).
- He prayed out loud for the benefit of the people there (vv. 41-2).
- He commanded in a loud voice, 'Lazarus, come out!' (v. 43).
- After Lazarus was raised he said, 'Take off the grave clothes and let him go' (v. 44).

Of course Jesus being the Son of God had a great deal of understanding that we do not have, especially in knowing what had happened to Lazarus and what he would be able to do when he reached Lazarus' home. The change in Jesus' thinking and feeling was nevertheless real.

Example 2

John is going shopping this morning. As he gets ready at home, he cannot find his wallet. He immediately jumps to the very worst conclusion that his wallet and credit cards have been stolen. He begins to feel very anxious, and notices a sick feeling in his stomach and a tense feeling in his head. He immediately phones the credit card agency and the bank to cancel all his cards. He then phones his friend Anne who he knows from his church Bible study group and talks to her for a few minutes to tell her what has happened. She is sympathetic and supportive, and encourages him to try and remember where he had last seen the wallet and suggests that he look around the house to see if he can find it. John thanks her and is pleased that he called her because he now feels a little better. He says he will let her know if he finds it and that he will see her that evening at her house for the next Bible study group meeting.

Later in the morning, John finds the wallet in his coat pocket. He had forgotten he had put it there yesterday. John then tries to avoid seeing or talking to Anne because he is worried that she will think that he is 'a right fool' and will ask him about this if he goes to the evening meeting. He therefore decides not to go to that evening's meeting as a result.

Q. How do John's *thoughts, physical/emotional reactions and behaviour* fit together? How does what he thought about the situation affect how he felt and what he did?

Q. What do you think of his interpretation of what had happened (immediately jumping to the very worst conclusion that the wallet was stolen and then later predicting that Anne will think badly of him, which is sometimes called 'mind-reading')?

Q. How could John have altered how he felt and what he did (immediately cancelling the cards and then avoiding Anne after he found the wallet again)?

Example 3

Anne is phoned by her friend John who is worried that he has lost his wallet. Anne knows that he has occasionally done this before and found the wallet later. Anne tries to tell John that it is possible he will find the wallet, and suggests he thinks back to when he last saw it and looks in places around the house such as in drawers, trousers and coat pockets. After John has rung off to go and do this, Anne begins to worry that she may have sounded irritable towards John and that she may not have been supportive enough. She feels guilty and worries that she has upset him, and later notices that he hasn't called her back to let her know what happened. John then also doesn't come to the Bible study meeting that she led that evening. That night, Anne lies awake worrying that their friendship has been harmed and that she has upset him. She decides not to phone John for a few days because she is not sure how he might react if she really has upset him.

Q. How do Anne's thoughts, physical/emotional reactions and behaviour fit together?

Q. Did her fear that she had upset John affect how she felt and what she did?

Yes ☐ No ☐

Q. How accurate were her fears that she had upset John?

Q. How did her worries alter her feelings?

Q. How could she have checked what John really thought?

In Examples 2 and 3, the person's fears (making *negative predictions* and *mind-reading* what the other person thought) led them to feel worse. Something that took only a short period of time (a few minutes on the phone) led to worry about what the other person thought of them for many of the following hours or days and affected how the person then reacted. In Anne's and John's case, in spite of this worry, neither of them actually phoned the other to check out how their friend had reacted. If they had, they would have realised quite how unhelpful and wrong their fears were.

Key point: What a person *thinks* affects *how they feel* physically and emotionally and alters *what they do*.

These examples also show that it is not necessarily the events themselves that cause upset, but the *interpretation* that people make of the event. In anxiety and depression, we tend to develop more extreme, negative and unhelpful thinking styles. These thoughts can build up out of all proportion, and unhelpfully affect how we feel and what we do.

THE IMPACT OF ANXIETY AND DEPRESSION ON THE FIVE AREAS

A Five Areas Assessment can be helpful in beginning to understand your symptoms of depression and anxiety. As you read through the following section, try to think about how what you read might apply to you.

Area 1: Situation, relationship and practical problems contributing to anxiety and depression

All of us from time to time face practical problems and difficulties. The actions of people around us can also create upsets and difficulties. Practical problems, such as relationship issues or financial difficulties, may also be present.

Are you facing any difficult situation, relationship or practical problems at the moment that may be linked to your own feelings of anxiety or depression? Write them here.

1. At home:

2. At work (or lack of work):

3. In my relationships:

a. With family/friends

b. With other church members/leaders

c. With God

4. Other practical problems (such as money, housing or other difficulties):

Your relationship with God

A very important aspect of understanding the impact of anxiety and depression on you as a Christian is to realise that distress affects our relationship with God. A common statement said by people who are feeling depressed or anxious is: 'The trouble is that not only do I feel constantly tired, fed up and worried, but it also seems as if

God has left me too. I have no joy or peace, and whereas once I used to feel God was very close to me, now he seems a million miles away.' So not only may we feel anxious or depressed, but suddenly God may seem remote too.

Do you feel like this at the moment? Yes ❑ No ❑

Bible example: The experience of feeling cut off from God seems to be the experience of the psalmist in Psalm 42.

> As a deer longs for flowing streams,
> so my soul longs for you, O God.
> My soul thirsts for God,
> for the living God.
> When shall I come and behold the face of God?
> My tears have been my food day and night,
> while people say to me continually,
> 'Where is your God?'
>
> I say to God, my rock,
> 'Why have you forgotten me?'
>
> (Psalm 42:1–3, 9a NRSV)

Not only did the psalmist, who once 'went with the throng, and led them in procession to the house of God' (v. 4b), feel the remoteness of a God he once had a close intimacy with, but he kept encountering people who contributed to his depressed mood by challenging the existence, or certainly the presence, of what was previously a source of comfort and strength.

So if you are feeling this way, be encouraged. Many great servants of God have travelled the same path and asked the same questions. But the question remains – why God should seem so remote when I feel like this and need him the most? One of the reasons why we can feel like this may be due to a false understanding of our own nature. We may have a picture of the human personality with different watertight compartments labelled 'Mind', 'Body' and 'Spirit' and, because we see these as different parts of our personality, we fail to understand how they relate to and interact with each other. Just because our mind or body is suffering we sometimes do not recognise that our spiritual life is likely to be affected too. The Bible does not describe different compartments of a human being; while Scripture speaks of the heart and the mind and the spirit of the individual it also recognises that we are a unity and each part of our existence affects, and is affected by, all of the others. Good physical health is likely to encourage good mental health, and both are likely to affect the spiritual aspects of our life; poor mental health may well go with poor physical health and both adversely affect how we feel and think about our relationship with God.

If you are feeling like this, Chapter 5, 'Maintaining your walk with God – practical things you can do that can make a difference', has been written for you.

Area 2: Altered thinking

When feeling low or anxious it is common to unhelpfully focus on events such as:

- *Past or current problems*. These can include practical difficulties such as debts, housing or neighbour problems, job or relationship difficulties or anything else you listed under Area 1. You may have self-critical thoughts in relation to a particular situation; what you or others have said, what others think of you and how you wish you or others had acted differently, etc.
- *Problems you may face in the future* (e.g. a job interview, unemployment, or how to deal with ongoing practical difficulties, such as debts, work or relationship problems). One of the less pleasant experiences for many people experiencing depression or anxiety is that the future looks

rather bleak and even hopeless. Usually it is not nearly as dark as most of us think at these times, but it frequently can seem as if there is no light at the end of the tunnel. At its worst, this may lead to thoughts of hopelessness, and even suicide.

Sometimes problems appear to completely dominate your thinking. It may seem as if you are using a telescope, which magnifies your problems and prevents you seeing any positive aspects of life. You may overlook or downplay your own strengths and ability to cope. You may believe you lack the capacity to overcome your problems, and that you have no chance of knowing how even to start to do so. The anxiety balance is upset, and you may begin to feel increasingly stressed and depressed as a result.

This *unhelpful* focus on problems and difficulties – past, present and future – does not help in sorting out your problems. Instead the problems are focused on and mulled over again and again in a way that doesn't help solve them, and may in fact make them seem a lot worse than they really are.

Anxiety and depression may also lead to other changes in how you think:

- Thoughts become *extreme* and it is common to get things out of all proportion.
- You may find that you make *negative predictions* about how things will work out and *jump to the very worst conclusion* that things have or will go very wrong.
- Like John and Anne, you may *mind-read* and second-guess that others think negatively of you, and rarely check out whether these fears are true.

- You may overlook your strengths or the positive aspects of a situation, and focus instead on times when you judge yourself as having failed or when things have gone badly wrong. You may become *overly self-critical* and unfairly feel responsible if things don't turn out well. Sometimes it can seem as if we are seeing things through a *negative mental filter* so that only the negatives in the situation and in ourselves are seen, and more positive aspects or personal strengths or supports are overlooked.

These changes in how we think are sometimes called unhelpful thinking styles.

Key point: Unhelpful thinking styles

These unhelpful thinking styles are important because they tend to reflect consistent and unhelpful thought patterns that we use again and again. Almost everyone shows at least some of these thinking styles from time to time. Normally when we are not feeling low or distressed, we can balance and challenge these thoughts fairly easily. The problem is that during times of anxiety and depression, they become more frequent, come into our minds more and become harder to challenge. Beginning to notice these thinking patterns is an important first step in the process of change and you will find out more about how to pick them up and then challenge them in Chapter 6.

Why are they called 'unhelpful' thinking styles?

Extreme thoughts are unhelpful because of their impact on you and others.

What you think can affect how you feel emotionally
Altered thinking with negative and extreme thoughts can make you feel worse. If you are always thinking other people don't like you or think that you're no good, or believe the future is really bleak, you are likely to quickly become disheartened and depressed.

Negative thinking ➡ Worsened mood

What you think can affect what you do
Negative thoughts may cause you to stop doing or avoid things that previously gave you a sense of pleasure or achievement, or to start doing things that actually worsen how you feel. For example, sometimes people may stop attending church, talking to God, visiting their friends or taking part in sporting activities. They may instead start doing things such as drinking to try and block how they feel, or stay indoors to avoid contact with people who they think do not like them very much.

Negative thinking ➡ Reduced/avoided activities or start unhelpful behaviours

You will find out more about this unhelpfully altered behaviour later in this chapter.

Our thoughts about God and our relationship with him
These unhelpful thinking styles are particularly important when we come to think about how they can alter our view not only of ourselves, but also of God, our relationship with him, and others in the Church.

Common thoughts and fears include:

- Remembering mistakes and sins from the past and dwelling on these excessively in ways that lead to self-condemnation and guilt.
- Thinking that you are cut off from God, or have displeased him,

or that you can no longer feel his presence as you did in the past.
- Thinking that others in the Church think badly of you, or that if you told them how you really felt, they would find you out and be critical of you/your faith as a Christian.
- Fearing that you had committed the 'unforgivable sin'.

We will look at these and other common fears in greater detail in the next chapter, and at ways of using your faith to overcome them.

Area 3: Altered mood

In anxiety and depression, we may notice changes in how we feel with:

Low mood

Common terms that people use to describe low mood include depression, or feeling low/sad/blue/upset/down/miserable/fed up. Typically in severe depression we feel excessively down and few, if any, things can pick us up from this feeling.

Feeling worse (more depressed or lower in mood) first thing in the morning

Mood that is worse in the morning and then improves as the day progresses can be a symptom of depression.

A profound lack of enjoyment or pleasure in things

In depression, things that previously would have been fun or given a sense of pleasure now seem to lack any enjoyment. Sometimes we may feel emotionless. In severe depression, almost nothing is enjoyed and it can seem that there are no emotions at all. For example, someone who normally would take great pleasure in worship music may find that they now have no pleasure when they listen to their tapes or take part in church services. The same may well be true of a whole range of social activity that previously gave a sense of fulfilment.

Guilt

In depression, we often feel terrible about letting ourselves or others down. We feel bad because we think we have failed against some legal or moral standard. Although at times guilt can be a helpful emotion to let us know when we have done something wrong, in depression our ability to feel healthy guilt is upset, and we may begin to feel excessively guilty, or guilty about things that we are not at all to blame for. You will read more about this 'false' guilt in Chapter 8.

Worry, stress, tension or anxiety

In worry, the person unhelpfully goes over things in their mind again and again. Doing this is not helpful because it doesn't help to solve the problems and generally makes them appear much worse – we lose perspective.

Panic

Sometimes levels of anxiety reach such a high level that we feel really panicky, very scared, or even terrified, believing that something catastrophic is about to happen right now. It may lead to hasty measures such as stopping what we are doing and running away. Such high levels of anxiety are unpleasant but not dangerous.

Anger or irritability with yourself or with others

Little things that normally wouldn't bother us seem to really irritate or upset us when we are feeling depressed or anxious. Anger tends to happen when someone breaks a rule that we believe is important, or acts to threaten or frustrate us in some way.

Ashamed or embarrassed at yourself or what you have done
Feeling ashamed of ourselves or our appearance can happen because we think ourselves to be inferior to others and fail to note our own achievements.

Q. Do you notice any of these changes in how you feel that may be linked to your own feelings of anxiety or depression? Write them here:

Area 4: Altered physical feelings/symptoms
Anxiety and depression affect all aspects of the person – mental and physical. Physical changes may include:

Altered sleep
Sleep changes commonly occur in depression. This can lead you to feel tired even after a night in bed. It can be more difficult getting off to sleep, and sometimes sleep is disrupted. Another common change is to waken in the early hours of the morning and not to be able to get off to sleep again.

Altered weight
Weight loss can occur as a result of reduced appetite. Sometimes weight gain can occur because of comfort eating and

reduced activity since fewer calories are burned up. For some people, weight gain can cause them to feel even worse about themselves.

Reduced energy
Low energy is a common problem and the person may feel tired all the time, and that they cannot do anything. As a result, in severe depression, things that previously would have seemed quite simple tasks, such as getting dressed or washed or going out, may become very difficult.

A reduced sex drive
Sex drive is often lost as part of depression or anxiety. A loss of libido is also a common symptom of anxiety and stress. Often this is an area the person feels unwilling to talk about, but may lead to further upset in close current relationships. Sex is sometimes an avoided topic in churches, and this may lead to further difficulties when trying to find someone to talk to about this.

Constipation or diarrhoea
Constipation can occur as part of the physical slowing down of the body that occurs in depression. Sometimes, constipation is worsened by antidepressants. In contrast, in anxiety a loosening of the bowels may occur with symptoms of diarrhoea and discomfort in the abdomen and stomach. If you are unsure about this, or if you have noticed any persistent change in your bowel habits, discuss it with your doctor.

Symptoms of pain
If you already have problems such as arthritis or other physical problems, depression and anxiety can often make it seem harder to cope. Pain can sometimes be an important symptom

of both depression and anxiety. They may cause tension headaches, or contribute to chest or stomach pains such as those causing an irritable bowel.

Physical agitation
Both anxiety and depression can lead to a marked increase in symptoms of physical tension. This may mean that the person finds it difficult to sit still. They may become restless and feel forced to get up and walk around, being unable to settle. This can cause particular difficulties in a church service where people usually sit down for lengthy periods of time, particularly during sermons.

Do you notice any physical changes that may be linked to your own feelings of anxiety or depression? Write them here:

Area 5: Altered behaviour
What we think affects what we do. Some changes of behaviour can unfortunately make matters worse, but others can help us feel better. There are two ways in which unhelpful behaviours may add to feelings of anxiety and depression:

1. *Stopping or reducing doing things* that are fun or give a sense of achievement and encouragement (e.g. going to church,

praying, meeting friends, hobbies, sports and other interests). This may include an avoidance of doing things or going to places that seem scary and cause anxiety when you feel vulnerable. For example, if you feel anxious in the company of large numbers of people, or have low levels of confidence, you may be tempted to avoid going to church services, which can appear to become quite scary.

2. *Starting to do activities which quickly become unhelpful* (e.g. beginning to drink to block how you feel, or choosing to lie in bed, isolating yourself/pushing away people who care).

Do you notice any changes in what you do that may be linked to your own feelings of anxiety or depression? Write them here:

You will find out more about this in Chapter 3.

A summary of how depression has affected you in the last week

The purpose of asking you to carry out the Five Areas Assessment isn't to demoralise you or to make you feel worse. Instead, by helping you consider how you are now, this can help you plan the areas you need to focus on to bring about change.

Task: Think about the impact of anxiety and depression on you over the last week or so. Use 'The Five Areas Assessment Model' on page 58 to summarise their current impact on you. Try to summarise all aspects of how you feel. Think about the impact on you, the people around you, and your relationship with God, your church leaders and the church itself. This might seem quite a difficult task at first, so feel able to do just a little and then come back to it after a while. If you find you cannot fill in each box then just do what you can and move on; you may be able to come back and fill in the gaps later.

Key point: By summarising your problems in this way, you have now identified clear problem areas to focus on changing. It is important to make sure that you do things one step at a time. A key to success is avoiding the temptation to throw yourself into tackling everything at once. *Slow steady steps* are more likely to result in improvement than very enthusiastically starting and then running out of steam.

The treatment of anxiety and depression

There are a range of approaches to treatment for anxiety and depression, and you will find out more about these in Chapter 9. One of them is Cognitive Behaviour Therapy (CBT). This helps look at the thoughts ('cognitions' – hence *cognitive*) and behaviours that might be adding to your problems. The approach focuses on working to overcome problems of anxiety and depression by:

1. Helping you to *challenge extreme and unhelpful thoughts* in order to help you get your thinking back into perspective. This will show

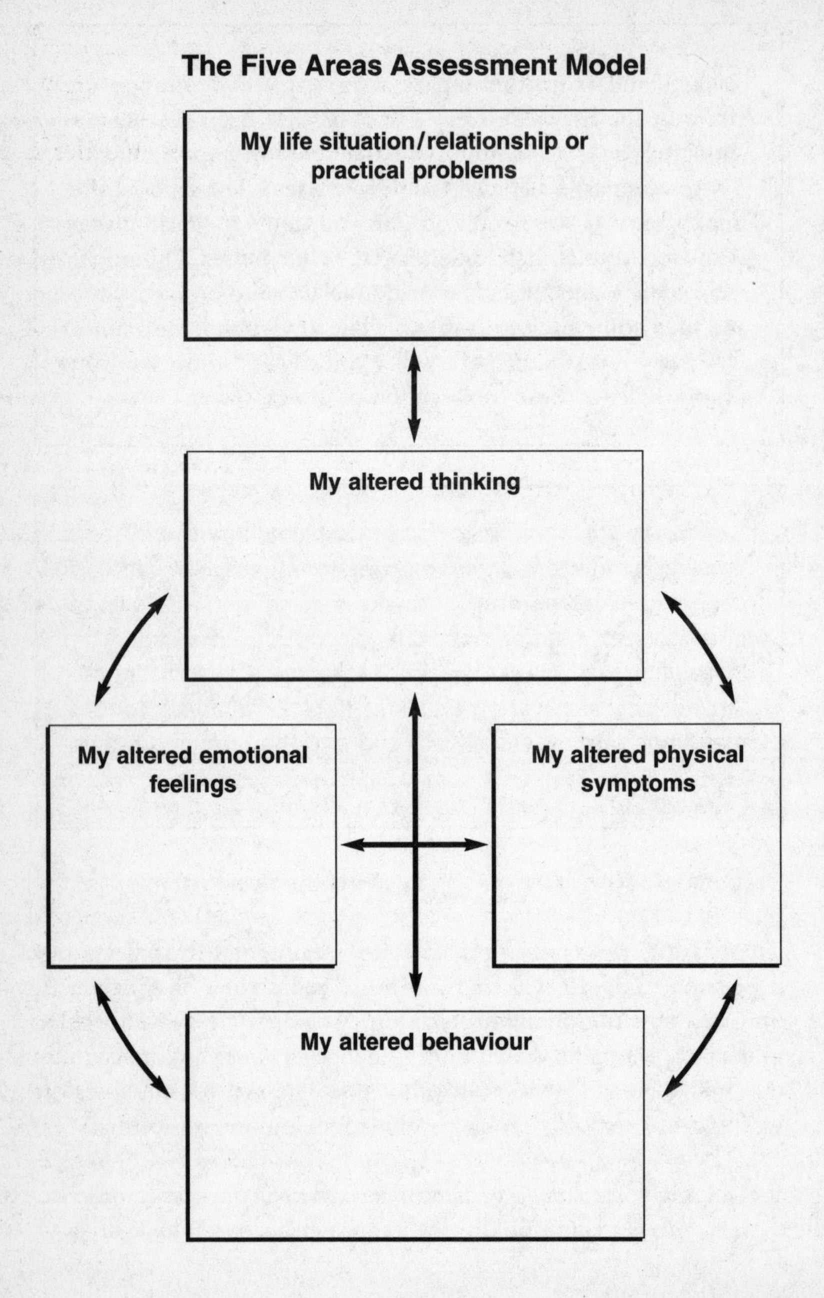
The Five Areas Assessment Model
My life situation/relationship or practical problems
My altered thinking
My altered emotional feelings
My altered physical symptoms
My altered behaviour

you how to stop dwelling on the worst possible things that could happen and to begin to see things more realistically. Prayer and seeking God's views on how he sees you and your current situation can be an important part of this process, and this is summarised in Chapters 5 and 8.

2. Helping you learn how to *reduce the physical symptoms of anxiety*. Learning effective relaxation approaches can help you do this. You may wish to buy a relaxation tape, or listen to Christian worship music, sounds of nature or other music that helps you to relax.
3. Tackling *reduced activity and avoidance* and reducing any *unhelpful coping behaviours* that are adding to your problems. An important part of overcoming depression and anxiety is to slowly build your confidence by starting to do those things that you have previously been avoiding. This should be done in a planned, step-by-step way, which will help you change little by little. You will find out more about this in Chapter 7.

Summary

The chapter has covered:

- A description of the main symptoms of anxiety, panic and depression.
- The five areas of anxiety and depression: the situations, relationships and practical problems faced by the person, and the altered thinking, emotional and physical feelings and behaviour that may occur.
- The unhelpful thinking styles and their impact on how you feel and what you do.
- The impact of anxiety and depression on you; helping you carry out your own Five Areas Assessment.
- The treatment of anxiety and depression using a CBT approach.

Putting into practice what you have learned

The important thing is to think about how you can put what you have learned into practice. We hope that one thing you have learned is that there are a great many people experiencing the same kind of distress as yourself. This should be something of a comfort – *you are not alone.* Because this is so, the prayer to finish this section has been written with all the other people suffering from anxiety or depression in mind. Pray this when you are able to, and then try to complete the tasks that follow over the next week or so.

CLOSING PRAYER

When you can, pray this prayer silently or preferably aloud.

Thank you, Father, that what I am feeling is not because I am worthless or inferior, and for the knowledge that many other people even now are feeling much as I am. I pray today especially for your people who are feeling worried and stressed, for those feeling cut off from you, depressed and even suicidal.

Thank you for your love for me and those sharing similar experiences just now. Thank you for caring for me, and for always being there, even when I do not feel as if you are. I pray for myself and for others using this book that we will know your healing and restoring presence. Help us to apply what we have learned to our everyday lives.

Help us to trust you, even when trusting anyone seems difficult.

I place my trust in you again.

I believe that the dark tunnel will come to an end in your time.

In the name of Jesus,

Amen.

Bible meditation

Meditate and pray about what Jesus has to say about the problems of life and worry in Matthew 6:25–34. As you do so, try to answer the following questions:

- What is helpful for me in this passage?
- What do God's promises say to me at this time?
- How can I hold on to these promises and keep them in my heart?
- What would prevent me taking hold of these promises for myself? What can I ask God to do in me to prevent this happening?
- What changes can I make myself to make sure I choose to focus on what he has to say?

Write the most helpful verses out and carry them around with you so that you can remind yourself of their truth when you need to. Alternatively, or additionally, read Matthew 6:25–34 through slowly each day for a week to allow its truths to sink in.

Also spend a few minutes with the following Bible passages, and allow God's thoughts and words to sink in. Try not to rush this.

- 'He will keep you strong to the end, so that you will be blameless on the day of our Lord Jesus Christ. God, who has called you into fellowship with his Son Jesus Christ our Lord, is faithful' (1 Corinthians 1:8–9).
- 'For this reason, since the day we heard about you, we have not stopped praying for you and asking God to fill you with the knowledge of his will through all spiritual wisdom and understanding . . . For he has rescued us from the dominion of darkness and brought us into the kingdom of the Son he loves, in whom we have redemption, the forgiveness of sins' (Colossians 1:9–14).

Key point: God loves us, wants the best for us and will not let us go.

Suggested points for action

Think who you are talking to about how you feel. Prayer support from other believers when we are depressed or anxious is very important. Our communication with God and fellow Christians is likely to make a big difference over time, but to receive this support we need to be willing to communicate what we are feeling, and right now this might be difficult for you. If you have not yet told anyone in your church of your depression or anxiety, try to think now of someone you can trust, preferably in a leadership position, who will promise to pray for you and perhaps encourage a few others you can trust to do the same over the coming weeks.

If you have any difficulties with these tasks, don't worry. Just do what you can.

My notes

3

The impact of unhelpful thinking and behaviour

The aim of this chapter is to help you consider in more detail the impact that anxiety and depression may be having on your thoughts and actions. It will help you to identify which chapters to read in Part 3 of the book.

Your unhelpful thinking styles

In anxiety and depression, it can sometimes seem that everything is viewed in a negative way. This might include:

A bias against yourself

Have you become very negative about yourself and full of self-blame and critical self-talk? Nothing you do is right, and you are your own worst critic?

Example

In Chapter 2 you read about John who had mislaid his wallet one morning, then found it and ended up not going to the Bible study group that night. He beat himself up mentally about not going and said to himself, 'I'm useless, I mess everything up.'

Putting a negative slant on things

Do you overlook or downplay the positive, and focus instead on the negative side of every situation? Does it seem that you have a mental filter that sees only the negative – 'a negative mental filter' – as if you are looking at everything through dark-tinted glasses?

Example

- Anne sits at home by herself feeling sad after the Bible study meeting has finished, and John has failed to attend. She thinks back to her phone conversation with him that morning and worries that she has upset him. She says to herself, 'The last week was completely awful. Nothing went right and I've completely messed up my friendship with John.'

You may know of similar experiences in your own life when you have filtered what you have seen and heard, and decided your worth was being undermined. Almost certainly this is because of the way you have filtered information.

Having a gloomy view of the future

Do you find yourself making negative predictions about the future and worry that the very worst will happen? This process of predicting that the very worst will happen is also called 'catastrophic thinking'. This may include a loss of hope, or even suicidal ideas.

Example

Going back to the story of Anne and John, it's next Sunday and John is at home at 9.30 a.m. The church service begins in half an hour. He thinks, 'I'm not going to go this morning – all my Bible study group will be there. They will be critical of me, I'll feel isolated and probably be told not to come back. The minister or an elder will "want a few words" and will tell me how inconsiderate I have been. I will have to try to explain why I wasn't there on Wednesday, and it will be really embarrassing.'

A negative view about how others see you

Another common, unhelpful thinking style in both anxiety and depression is second-guessing or mind-reading that others don't like you or see you as weak, stupid or useless. Usually, the person does not actually try to find out if their fears are true.

Example

- John finally decides to go to church, but deliberately sits at the back near the door. Throughout the service he worries about what others will say to him. He mind-reads that 'they will think I'm an idiot and a waste of time'. At the end of the service he gets up quickly and leaves.
- Mark sees his pastor speaking to a group of people and walks across, demanding to know why they are discussing him; in fact he was not even mentioned in the conversation.

Bearing all responsibility

Have you noticed that you often feel guilty and unfairly take responsibility for things? Do you feel the pressure for things to go well, and blame yourself if things don't go as expected, even if you are not to blame (e.g. 'I'll ruin the evening for everybody and it will all be my fault')? An example that many people can identify with is the experience of feeling responsible for everyone else having a good time if you invite some friends round for a meal or a party. The person is prone to take things to heart. In anxiety and depression, the person often feels unfairly responsible for things that are nothing really to do with them, and they feel like this a lot of the time.

Example

During the service Anne notices John at the back of church. She feels guilty that she may have upset him by being irritated with him when he phoned up, saying he had lost his wallet. The numbers have been slightly down at the study group and Anne starts thinking, 'I'm not offering the right sort of supportive relationship there for people as the study group leader. It's all my fault that John didn't come on Wednesday.' She then notices that he has left church before she has a chance to talk to him.

Making extreme statements or rules

In this type of unhelpful thinking style, very strong statements are made, e.g. 'It was completely useless', even when what actually happened wasn't anywhere near that bad. Do you set yourself impossible targets that no one could possibly meet (e.g. 'It must be completely perfect, anything less will mean total failure')? This thinking style causes the person to use the words 'should', 'got to', 'must' and 'ought' a lot, and also to use very strong statements including words such as 'always' and 'never' (e.g. 'I never do things right'), and 'typical' (e.g. 'Just typical, everything always goes wrong').

Example

Anne says to herself, 'As the study group leader, I *must* do my very best to make sure that everyone in the group feels God's presence. If they don't grow as a Christian then I've totally failed as the leader and I'll have let God down in the work he has called me to do. I've got to work harder at this.'

Task: Think back over the last week. Have you noticed any of these unhelpful thinking styles?

Summary of my unhelpful thinking styles over the last week

Unhelpful thinking style	**Typical thoughts**	**Tick here if you have this thinking style and write down an example**
1. Bias against myself	I overlook my strengths. I focus on my weaknesses. I downplay my achievements. I am my own worst critic.	
2. Putting a negative slant on things (negative mental filter)	I see things through dark tinted glasses. I tend to focus on the negative in situations.	
3. Having a gloomy view of the future (make negative predictions/jump to the worst conclusion – catastrophising)	I make negative predictions about the future. I predict that things will go wrong.	
4. Negative view about how others see me (mind-reading)	I mind-read what others think of me. I often think that others don't like me.	
5. Bearing all responsibility	I feel responsible for whether everyone else has a good time. I take things to heart. I take the blame if things go wrong. I take unfair responsibility for things that are not my fault.	
6. Making extreme statements/rules	I use the words 'always', 'never' and 'typical' a lot to summarise things. I make 'must', 'should' or 'ought' statements to myself.	

Most people who will have completed the task on page 68 will have ticked at least one of the boxes. Some readers will have ticked several or most of the boxes. The more you have noticed, the more likely you are to interpret things in ways that may worsen how you feel and have an unhelpful impact on what you do.

Key point: These unhelpful thinking styles are common and normal. In everyday life, most of us think in these ways at least some of the time. Normally, such thoughts are relatively easily challenged, or only make up a small part of our thinking. However, in anxiety and depression these thoughts come into our minds more often, are harder to challenge and overcome, and cause much more distress. You may notice that you are more prone to one of these unhelpful thinking styles than others.

The impact of unhelpful thinking styles

Read the table below to find out more about the links between the different situations, thoughts, feelings and behaviour.

Situation, relationship or practical problem	Altered thinking	Emotional and/or physical impact	Unhelpful thinking style	Behaviour change
1. Anne calls by on John after church to find out why he has missed the last two study groups.	John: 'I've upset Anne and let her down.'	Feel low and guilty. Physical symptoms of distress.	Mind-reading and second-guessing that Anne thinks John has let her down. In fact she is concerned that she may have upset him.	John avoids eye-contact as he talks to Anne. He cuts the conversation short and tries to make Anne want to leave.

Situation, relationship or practical problem	Altered thinking	Emotional and/or physical impact	Unhelpful thinking style	Behaviour change
2. Next Wednesday, John is due to go to the next Bible Study group that is to be led by Anne.	John: 'It will go terribly. People will ask where I was last week. I'll be really embarrassed.'	Anxiety and physical symptoms of stress.	Make negative predictions. Jump to the worst conclusions.	Don't go. Avoidance.
3. Anne asks if someone will open the meeting with prayer. No one says anything.	Anne: 'It's all gone wrong. I'm a useless leader, I'm no longer up to the job.'	Feel low and notice physical symptoms of anxiety.	Bias against oneself.	Jumps in after thirty seconds and prays herself.
4. Next Sunday Anne listens to the morning sermon. The preacher says, 'We must all try our very best to fulfil the roles that God calls us to.'	Anne: 'I can't do it – people aren't growing as they should do. I can't lead the group. Look at what's happened with John, I really let him down.'	Feels low and very guilty with low energy and a lack of enthusiasm.	Bias against oneself. Feeling overly responsible/ taking things to heart.	Goes home and cries. Feels cut off from God, and that she is unusable by him. Phones to tell the minister that she is resigning from leading the study group.

While these episodes are taken from the everyday life of a church, the lessons to be learned apply to a wide variety of situations.

You can see from the table above that there are links between:

Negative thinking ➡ Worsened mood
Negative thinking ➡ Reduced/avoided activities or the start of unhelpful behaviour

UNHELPFULLY ALTERED BEHAVIOUR IN ANXIETY AND DEPRESSION

Reduced activity and avoidance

When people feel depressed or anxious, it is normal for them to find it is difficult doing things. This is because of:

- Low energy and tiredness ('I'm too tired/exhausted').
- Low mood and little sense of enjoyment or achievement when things are done.
- Anxiety and fear of doing particular things – for example, going shopping or talking to people.
- Negative thinking and reduced enthusiasm to do things ('I just can't be bothered').
- Perhaps feeling guilty about what they are experiencing, and think that they do not deserve any pleasure.

It can sometimes feel as though everything is too much effort or is just too difficult. A *vicious circle of reduced/avoided activity* may result. We use the term 'vicious circle' because in effect these factors combine with each other to deepen the depression and constantly lower our mood.

The result of this vicious circle is that the person begins to stop doing things. Soon even the everyday core things such as getting up and dressed, housework, driving, essential jobs, and looking after themselves feel more than they can cope with. In this way the circle of reduced/avoided activity becomes a downward spiral, and each time the circle is completed the person feels worse about themselves and their circumstances.

To help identify the impact of reduced activity/avoidance on you, answer the questions on page 73:

A Vicious Circle of Reduced Activity (in Depression) or Avoidance (in Anxiety) May Result

Depression or anxiety with:

- Low/anxious mood.
- Low energy and fatigue.
- Unhelpful thinking styles and reduced motivation *('I just can't be bothered')*.
- Fears *('I can't do that!')*.
- Feeling emotionally distant from God.

Difficulty doing things

Reduced activity: stop going out or meeting people. Stop hobbies and things that were fun. Find reading the Bible and praying difficult.

Avoidance of things that seem scary or too difficult. Avoid specific situations/people/places.

Reduced activity of things that lead to fun/pleasure and a sense of achievement

Reduced activity prevents you from doing potentially helpful things (such as going to mid-week groups/church, meeting with friends, going for walks, etc.). You only do essential jobs.

Avoidance saps your confidence further and restricts places/people/things you are able to do/meet.

Worsen feelings of depression or anxiety

a. Remove pleasure from life
Life becomes emptier and nothing is done that leads to enjoyment. Even essential jobs become too much effort.

b. Life becomes increasingly restricted
Become isolated and lose confidence with others/self. Possibly lose important sources of support. Avoidance leads to an increasingly restricted life ruled by fears.

Q. What things have I stopped doing because of my feelings of anxiety and/or depression?
Write here the things that used to give me a sense of *pleasure* or *achievement*:

Q. Write here other activities that were a source of support for me (friends, talking to others, going to church/study groups, talking about how I feel to others):

Q. Overall, does reduced activity or avoidance have an unhelpful effect on me? Yes ❑ No ❑

You will find out how to overcome this vicious circle in Chapter 7.

Unhelpful activities

When somebody becomes anxious or depressed, it is normal to try to do things that aid recovery. This altered behaviour may be *helpful* or *unhelpful*.

Helpful activities may include:

- Turning to friends inside or outside your church for support.
- Reading or using self-help materials to find out more about the causes and treatment of anxiety or depression.
- Going to see your doctor or health care practitioner to discuss what treatments may be helpful for you.
- Maintaining activities that provide pleasure or support such as going to church, reading the Bible, meeting friends, playing sport and engaging in outdoor pursuits.

Sometimes, however, the person may try to block how they feel with *unhelpful behaviour*. These are often extreme, for example:

Excessively telling others about your problems

At one extreme, the person may choose not to talk at all about how they feel. Keeping your problems to yourself may be because of a belief that 'Christians shouldn't have emotional problems', or that 'it is a sign of weakness to be stressed'. This is discussed later in this chapter.

At the other extreme, the person may recurrently seek support and excessive reassurance about their faith and the certainty of their relationship with God from trusted church members or leaders. This is a good example of an action that in moderation can be helpful and a source of support, but which can become unhelpful when taken to excess. The result is a feeling of dependency on others and a reinforcement of thoughts that others can communicate more readily with God than you can yourself. The result is a further loss of confidence in your relationship with God.

Recurrent repentance for the same sin

Having doubts about your faith and relationship with God – for example, doubting whether you are loved or truly forgiven – are common in anxiety and depression. Intrusive memories of sinful past actions may come to mind, and these can lead to recurrent bouts of self-criticism, repeated repentance and confession of the same sin. This can lead to responding again and again to invitations to recommit your life to Christ, bursting out in tears over and over again in church services or house groups, and simply an inability to move on from a problem that comes back to trouble you over and over again.

Of course these things are not unhealthy in themselves. The Bible positively encourages turning from wrongdoing, and it is encouraging that most churches are able to accept and help those who express strong emotion from time to time. Nevertheless it is important that we try to reach a point where we accept that, however we are feeling, God has forgiven us and removed our sin as far from us as the east is from the west (Psalm 103:12).

In one of her books Corrie Ten Boom illustrates what often happens when Christians ask God for forgiveness. She says that when they do that, it is as if God buries our sin at the bottom of the ocean. In spite of the fact that God has totally dealt with it, however, we sometimes rush to find our fishing rods and try to dredge it up again. She says that we need to put up a sign saying, 'No fishing!' This can be especially difficult to do when we are experiencing depression or anxiety, since we may well be quite capable of reading what the Bible says and still be convinced that we are the one exception to the rule.

Over-committing yourself to church work or withdrawing from it completely

At one extreme, sometimes when people feel anxious or depressed, they decide to totally stop going to church, reading the Bible, etc. and choose to do other things instead (e.g. stay in, watch television, do the decorating, or some of the things mentioned below). This matter will be addressed in Chapter 8, dealing with how to get the most from your church.

At the other extreme, sometimes the person may throw themselves into excessive church work, or into work in other settings such as home or the office/factory. The person attempts to 'work' themselves out of their distress, and becomes increasingly busy – filling every part of their day in order to avoid noticing quite how bad they feel. This may involve other ways of avoiding their emotional distress, such as deliberately staying up late watching films, or sleeping in during the day in order to avoid seeing others.

Another extreme reaction is seen occasionally when the person may be tempted to try to resolve their feelings by deliberately turning against their church or its members – questioning the faith of others, being angry, gossiping, spreading rumours, becoming bitter and critical, especially towards leaders who are easy targets and less likely to hit back. They may also turn against God (e.g. by seeing him as unloving or rejecting), and stop reading the Bible and praying. They may choose actively to cut themselves off from God by acting in a way that they know is against his will – having an affair, becoming obsessed by pornography, spending money only on themselves, starting to drink excessively, etc. When someone does this, it can sometimes seem as if they are testing out whether God really loves them, or as if they are proving to themselves that they are unlovable or unable to cope.

Using other unhelpful ways of blocking emotions

Sometimes people try to block their emotions by:

- Using alcohol or illegal drugs.
- Trying to spend their way out of depression/anxiety by visiting the shops and buying new clothes/goods in order to cheer themselves up.
- Harming themselves (by cutting or scratching arms, legs or stomach) as a way of blocking how they feel.

- Deliberately cutting themselves off from all their friends by being rude or irritable.
- Becoming very promiscuous.
- Acting in ways designed to set themselves up to fail and push others away. This may further worsen how they feel by ultimately increasing self-condemnation and confirming negative beliefs about themselves or others.

A vicious circle or spiral of unhelpful behaviour can result.

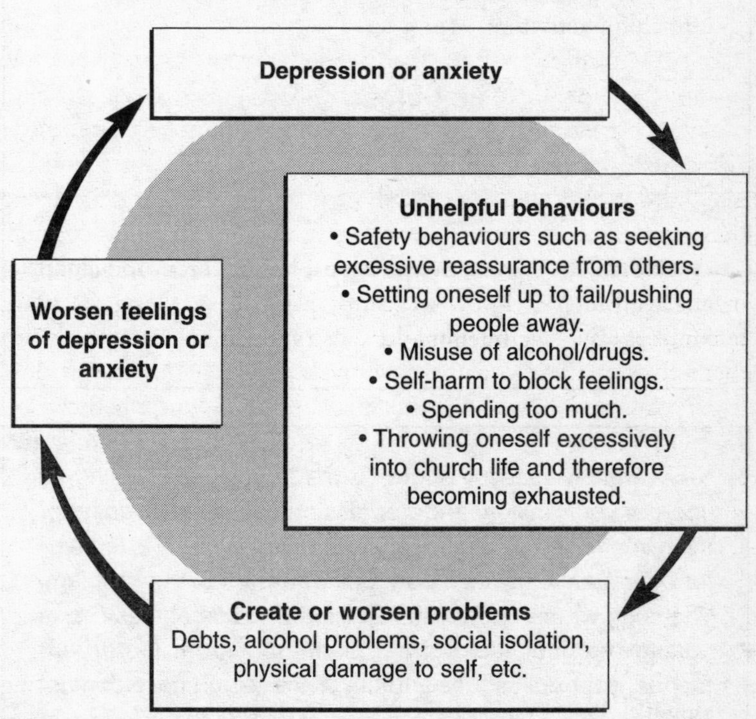

To help you to identify the impact of unhelpful behaviours answer the following questions:

Q. What things have I started doing in order to try to cope with or block my emotions? Write them here:

Helpful activities:

Unhelpful activities:

Q. Overall, do these activities have a helpful or an unhelpful effect on me?
Helpful ❑ Unhelpful ❑ Neutral ❑

Key point: Whatever originally made you start feeling as you do, your anxiety and depression can be kept going or even intensified by the *unhelpful thinking styles* and *unhelpful behaviour* that have now become part of the problem. They can worsen how you feel, and can sometimes cause you to feel isolated from your church, from God, your friends, your colleagues and anyone else you have contact with.

SUMMARY

This chapter has covered:

- Unhelpful thinking styles, and how you can identify them.
- The impact of these unhelpful thinking styles on how people feel and what they do, and how these can become part of the problem by keeping anxiety and depression going.
- The impact of removing things from life that otherwise would provide you with support or give you a sense of pleasure and/or achievement. This is described as the 'vicious circle of reduced/avoided activity'.
- The impact of beginning new behaviour (often extreme) that actually worsens your problems in the long term. This is described as the 'vicious circle of unhelpful behaviour'.

Putting into practice what you have learned
The important thing is to think about how you can put what you have learned into practice. One way is by praying this prayer and then completing the following tasks over the next week or so.

CLOSING PRAYER

When you can, pray this prayer silently or preferably aloud.

Lord, thank you for your love for me. I've learned lots of different things as I've read this chapter. I pray that you will let one or two things really sink into my heart and help me to make some changes in what I think and do.

Lord, I realise that many of the ways I have been seeing and judging things recently haven't been as you want them to be. At times I've been very negative, and have become very biased against myself and others. I have looked at myself and seen failure.

Thank you, Lord, that you look at me and see someone you love. Help me please to accept that you love me, and will continue to work in me to bring me back to full health. I pray that you will help me to make changes in how I think and in what I do so that I can begin to see things in more helpful ways and be restored to being a useful servant for you, learning to relax in your love for me.

Father, please help me to act in ways that allow others to support me; please help me to trust others enough to confide in those I need to share with about how I am without becoming too dependent on them. Help me not to push others away or act in ways that worsen how I feel.

Finally, Father, I remember the other readers of this book, who are struggling with similar problems. Help them as they also pray this prayer to know that you are answering it, and provide them with an inner assurance that you will stick with them through all things. I ask this in Jesus' name.

Amen.

Bible meditation

Remind yourself of what the Bible says and focus on this when you notice any of your old, unhelpful thinking styles.

- 'For you did not receive a spirit that makes you a slave again to fear, but you received the Spirit of sonship. And by him we cry "*Abba*, Father." The Spirit himself testifies with our spirit that we are God's children. Now if we are children, then we are heirs – heirs of God and co-heirs with Christ, if indeed we share in his sufferings in order that we may also share in his glory' (Romans 8:15–17).
- 'For I am convinced that neither death nor life, neither angels nor demons, neither the present nor the future, nor any powers, neither height nor depth, nor anything else in all creation, will

be able to separate us from the love of God that is in Christ Jesus our Lord' (Romans 8:38–9).

Try to remember that these promises and assurances are for you. The words of the Bible have God's authority and power; reading and saying them helps to establish their truth in your life.

Meditate about *each* of the passages above. As you do, try to answer the following questions:

- What is helpful for me in this passage?
- What does God say to me particularly at this time?
- How can I hold onto his promises and keep them in my heart?
- What could prevent me taking hold of these promises for myself? What can I ask God to do in me to prevent this happening?
- What changes can I make to my thought life and my behaviour to make sure I choose to focus on what he has to say?

Write out the most helpful passages and carry them around with you or pin them to your fridge door or notice-board so that you can remind yourself of their truth when you need to.

My notes

4

What are the causes of my anxiety and depression?

Having read the last chapter you may be keen to move on immediately to thinking about what you can do to overcome your unhelpful thinking styles and altered behaviour. This is the focus of Part 3 of this book.

While it is certainly important to address these issues, at this point we want to stop and reflect a little before moving on to think about how to make changes to the way we think and behave.

Why we think and act as we do in anxiety and depression

So what are the causes of these unhelpful thinking styles and behaviour? A number of psychological (thinking) factors are important in considering the cause of anxiety and depression. Sometimes extreme and unhelpful thinking can be started or worsened by a loss event (e.g. the breakdown of a relationship, loss of a job), or the threat of such a loss occurring. This may involve severe upsets in relationships – for example with a wife, husband, friends, or children.

Alternatively there may be long-term stresses – caused, for example, by living in cold and damp housing or by problems at work. Sometimes the cause of stress can be related to problems at church – for example, arguments about the style of services or the music and worship, or leadership style. Church relationship problems are often caused by a clash of personalities, particularly when leadership personnel changes. Most of us find that we can deal with a single problem; when one difficulty seems to follow another in a continuous pattern, however, or if just one very large upset occurs, almost anyone can feel overwhelmed and anxiety or depression can easily result.

In the Christian world any number of these difficulties may be attributed to 'spiritual' causes; expressions such as 'The devil's having a field day' or 'Satan is really attacking us' may be common currency. We have no wish to deny the reality of spiritual warfare, which is discussed in Chapter 10. However much malicious spiritual forces are involved in a particular situation, though, the real issues are often initially human ones, albeit sometimes twisted and manipulated by forces of darkness to damage the effectiveness of individual Christians and local churches. As we shall see in Chapter 8, it is unbiblical and generally unhelpful to classify every problem – inside or outside the Church – as only 'spiritual' or 'non-spiritual', as most problems in churches have both human and spiritual dimensions. Psychological factors are still very important in understanding how people react in unhelpful ways to each other and to various situations.

People are very different in how they respond to loss events and to the different forms of stress that they face. One key factor is the importance of *our inner rules* that we learn as we grow up.

Our inner rules

As we grow up, we each learn important rules about how we understand and make sense of ourselves and the people and events around us. It is in childhood that these central ways of seeing things are first learned. They will be largely determined by our relationships with people who are important to us – especially our parent or parents, brothers and sisters, and to a lesser extent by our wider family and friends.

These central ways of seeing things are sometimes called 'core beliefs'. Common core beliefs may be based around positive themes such as seeing yourself as competent and successful, or more unhelpful themes such as being a failure, bad, unlovable, incompetent, foolish or weak. Most people learn a range of both positive and negative core beliefs during their childhood. Even if someone has a very happy upbringing, it is common for them to have at least some unhelpful beliefs about how they see themselves or others. Even if someone is not usually troubled by negative and unhelpful core beliefs, if they develop depression or anxiety the few they have may still come to dominate their thinking and lead to a wide range of extreme and unhelpful ways of thinking and acting. What is more, we will usually fail to see that this is a symptom of depression and believe that our self-evaluation is not only true, but entirely separate from our condition. The good news is that no matter how difficult our background has been, or how varied our unhelpful inner rules are, God still loves us unconditionally and can help us to learn new core beliefs – the knowledge of being loved, forgiven, supported and saved.

As well as learning these different 'rules' as we grow up at home and in society, we also learn different 'rules' in the churches we go to, through discussion, teaching, reading and the church culture that we are exposed to over the years. One of the main motivating factors in writing this book has been the belief that whereas our Christian faith should be a major asset in overcoming depression and anxiety it is not infrequently the case that the way supposed spiritual values are expressed by ourselves and others can unfortunately produce exactly the opposite effect.

PROBLEM ATTITUDES THAT ARE COMMON AMONG CHRISTIANS

We spoke earlier about common unhelpful core beliefs that we may have learned as we grew up. We continue to learn new 'rules' throughout our lives, and sometimes unfortunately the rules we learn in church can also become unhelpful. These are some of the most common unhelpful rules that we as Christians can learn within our churches and in the wider Christian world.

1. We must be 'perfect' Christians

As Christians we are sometimes prone to extreme or black and white thinking. This is sometimes called 'all or nothing' thinking because it describes the tendency of people who think in this way to shift quickly from one emotional state to another. It can be unhelpful for us as Christians because it can rapidly lead us to states of self-condemnation, excessive guilt and self-recrimination.

Example 1

Mark is a 32-year-old Christian who works as a secondary school teacher. He has always been prone to set himself high standards and continued to do this after he became a Christian. He often sets himself rules, using terms like 'I must/should/ought to . . .' and often thinks to himself that he has 'got to' do things right. After a particularly good Sunday he begins Monday morning feeling victorious as a Christian and especially close to God; he received prayer ministry after the service last evening, left church on a spiritual 'high', and is sure that in spite of previous failures, this week will be different. He has the right attitude towards his pupils and deals with them well. His pre-prepared lesson plans also seem to be effective. He thanks God for this and is sure that he will be a good witness throughout the week. In the final lesson of the day, though, tired from a busy schedule, he briefly shouts at a pupil who is talking loudly to others at the back of the classroom. This causes great problems for Mark as he has violated his personal rule that as a Christian, 'I shouldn't get angry or raise my voice.' His reaction as a result is not to ask himself calmly if that was the best way of dealing with the situation, but to judge himself as having totally failed as a Christian. He feels cut off from God, and goes home thinking that he is an utter failure in his Christian witness. This feeling continues for the rest of the week, and his sense of self-worth spirals downwards.

Example 2

Sandra is a 38-year-old housewife, and mother of three children – two at school and a 2-year-old toddler at home. Her husband works at a factory ten miles away, for which he needs to use the family car. In order to provide the family with holidays and other odd luxuries Sandra works twenty hours every week as a bookkeeper, while her mother looks after the toddler. Life for Sandra is a constant juggling act, trying to stay on top of the various jobs that make up her life. She tries to do her paid work well, is never late and always smartly dressed. Sandra has read Proverbs 31 with its view of the ideal wife and mother, and is determined always to live by its precepts. She also believes that since her own mother kept the house in a state of immaculate tidiness, with meals cooked on time every day, freshly baked cakes in the cupboard and a constant supply of clean, dry and ironed clothes, that a good Christian housewife should keep her home looking immaculate. In addition she considers it really important to read with all three children every school day, and be available to listen to Mike, her husband, when he comes in from work feeling that he has had a hard day. As a committed Christian she feels she must contribute to the life of the church, so helps with the Mums and Tots group as well as teaching in Sunday school.

Life for Sandra is one long struggle to juggle all these 'balls' and keep them in the air at the same time. Against the odds she more-or-less succeeds, until she falls ill with a virus. While Sandra is struggling to keep job, home, family and church all going in some fashion, Steve, the minister of her church, drops in to chat about Sunday school. Seeing a pile of crockery piled up in the kitchen he comments, 'Looks like you could do with a dishwasher.' The remark is intended light-heartedly and in no sense as a criticism. What Sandra hears, however, is, 'This house is in an absolute mess. What sort of Christian wife and mother do you call yourself when you allow things to get in this state?'

What has happened is that Sandra's personal rule (largely inherited from her mother, who did not have to go out to work) that 'a good Christian housewife should keep her home looking immaculate' has been violated. This sense of failure, combined with her physical illness, causes her mood to drop and she begins to feel depressed. It is all she can do to keep going to work and cook dinner each day. When she cannot find time or energy to read with the children she feels a complete failure as a mother too. Because she becomes very tired and has a low mood she does not feel like making love to her husband either, and so she brands herself as a failure as a wife.

Before many days have passed Sandra is simply not coping with the housework or children, and her work is suffering. She avoids making an appointment with her doctor because she is afraid of being prescribed antidepressants, but feels her mood constantly dropping. Her Sunday-school work suffers next as she has insufficient time or energy to prepare it properly, and as God seems remote she now considers herself a failure as a Christian as well.

Sandra's difficulties were created because two or three internalised rules to do with what a good Christian wife and mother is like were broken. She tried to model her everyday life on the idealised picture of womanhood in Proverbs 31, and to follow the example of her own mother. It would have been perfectly reasonable to say that when she contracted a virus she needed help, could not do all her jobs well and would probably need some time off work, but her own inner rules would not permit her to do so. Just one chance remark began a downward spiral of altered thinking and behaviour that led to severe depression.

Similarly, in Mark's case his unhelpful style of thinking had a bad effect on how he felt for the rest of the week even though he had barely raised his voice, and on reflection it was reasonable to challenge a pupil who is disrupting the lesson for others. Nevertheless all the good feelings gained from the previous Sunday were lost as a result of his determination to impose unreasonable standards on himself.

Here are some other examples of extreme black and white/all or nothing rules:

- 'I must always stand up for my faith.'
- 'I must pray and read the Bible for twenty minutes every day.'
- 'I must never miss church.'
- 'I must be a perfect wife and mother/husband and father.'
- 'I must always respond positively when someone asks for help.'
- 'I must always do what a church leader asks me to do.'

Any failure to meet these targets may lead to excessive feelings of failure and sometimes great despair. High standards can be helpful if held to a moderate degree, but can backfire and have an unhelpful impact on how we feel and what we do at times when we have problems meeting these standards (as, for example, often occurs during periods of anxiety or depression). At such times we find it increasingly hard to maintain these standards, and the result is that we beat ourselves up mentally and see ourselves as failing.

Part of the difficulty in this area for Christians is that preachers and leaders often call for greater levels of commitment, and use biblical heroes as examples of what we should all be like. While on one level trying to emulate characters from the Bible is a worthy target, we can be left with the impression that we are being asked to do something we are simply not capable of, and therefore that we are a failure in our own and God's sight. Of course the Bible does set high standards for our conduct, attitude and commitment. Paul spoke in these terms about the Christian life: 'But one thing I do: Forgetting what is behind and straining towards what is ahead, I press on towards the goal to win the prize for which God has called me heavenwards in Christ Jesus' (Philippians 3:13b–14). This call to commitment, holiness and pursuit of God is, however, balanced by God's incredible capacity to be gracious and forgiving, and to restore those who fall.

There are probably some reading this book who seriously wonder if it is possible for God to restore and forgive them, given what they have done in the past. It is worth remembering that some of the greatest men and women of God in the Bible made absolutely catastrophic mistakes. King David, for example, not only committed adultery with Bathsheba, but murdered her husband in order to do so (2 Samuel 11–12). Even so, he discovered that God forgave him, and can restore those who have fallen in the most spectacular ways.

God is both merciful and gracious. 'Mercy' refers to God's willingness to withhold punishment that we deserve, and 'grace' is God's capacity to give what we do not deserve. If you are feeling that you have failed so badly that God cannot possibly forgive you or, if he has forgiven you, that he has little further interest in you, then these feelings are just that – feelings – that contradict the character of God that is revealed in the Bible. If you are thinking like this, you may find it helpful to read through Psalm 51 – which was possibly based on the disastrous mistake David made with Bathsheba – and make it your own prayer.

Key point: You can see from these examples that although on one level these 'rules' are often biblical ones, black and white styles of thinking do not reflect the whole truth of Scripture, where a call to holiness and purity is balanced by the inexhaustible capacity of God to be gracious and forgiving. The danger with black and white thinking is that it results in rapid self-condemnation when we fail to live up to our own self-imposed rules, resulting in rapidly swinging moods and making us quickly feel totally defeated. These rules are unhelpful because must/should/ought standards can never be completely kept and impose commitments we cannot possibly keep. They are unrealistic because they do not allow sufficiently for human weaknesses or the realities of life. Significantly, instead of our faith being part of the solution to our problems it has become part of the problem itself. This does not water down the call of Scripture to be wholly set apart and available for God's use, but presents a more balanced view of how God deals with us in grace and mercy, as well as in a call to holiness and commitment.

You may notice that you also hold similar extreme rules about other areas of life, and if you think back you may realise that you were prone to hold these sorts of rules even before you became a Christian. These unhelpful must/should/ought rules are almost certainly more to do with you and your background than they are to do with how God wants you to live the Christian life.

Task: Think about the reaction of Jesus to those around him who were sinners. Consider how Jesus reacted to the woman caught in adultery as described in John 8:1-11: ' "Then neither do I condemn you", Jesus declared. "Go now and leave your life of sin" ' (v. 11). What are the implications of his statement in verse 11 for you now?

Key point: Jesus never focused only on the person's sin; instead he balanced this with statements that God loved and forgave them and showed them that they could change. Grace always had the last word. In John 8 compare his attitude to the woman caught in adultery with his approach to the Pharisees and other religious leaders who maintained the highest imaginable levels of adherence to their laws, but who were guilty of things like pride and hypocrisy.

God does not overwhelm us with judgment but prompts us to change at a pace we can cope with, and usually this is fairly slow. By doing this we will save ourselves a lot of anxiety and self-condemnation. He knows what is best for us and wants us to grow because he loves us. He does not condemn us or point out our failings in ways that undermine us, but accepts us and draws us into an ever deeper relationship with himself, while at the same time gently challenging areas of sin and disobedience in our lives.

If you have become a Christian quite recently, the realisation of what God asks of us in terms of moral standards and commitment may have come as something of a shock to the system. God will be incredibly patient with you as you adjust to a completely new way of seeing the world, so don't be alarmed if the lifestyle changes you now know are right do not happen all at once. Do not beat yourself up with what still needs to be changed, but allow the Holy Spirit to deal with each area of your life as and when he sees fit.

2. We are lop-sided with *either* a 'feeling' *or* a 'thinking' faith

Some of what follows might appear to be a caricature of what church is really like; we cannot possibly cover every type of church in addressing this issue, but we hope that you will be able to understand the point we are trying to make. Each body of believers has its own distinctive style, and no two fellowships are exactly alike, but for the purposes of this chapter it will be helpful if we can see church life as broadly *feeling*-oriented or *fact*-oriented. The intention is not to say that one approach is superior to the other – the authors come from different types of fellowships in this sense anyway – but to try to understand how the outworking of our faith can become lop-sided in emphasising either the brain or the heart. In reality most church leaders aim to strike a healthy balance between the two, even though one may predominate over the other.

Feeling-oriented churches may seem to concentrate more on our individual experience of God, exuberance in worship and close personal relationships within the church. The feeling/emotional side of faith may be strongly emphasised, with the more intellectual side of faith taking something of a back seat. An emphasis is often placed on the experience of God, and living life as a Christian today. Put simply, the heart seems to be seen as of greater significance than the head.

In contrast *fact-oriented churches* place their main focus on the mind and understanding, and emphasise the academic and intellectual aspects of faith. These churches may stress the need for 'right' doctrine, and offer lengthy and detailed doctrinal teaching that may have less application to relationships and the experience of God.

It is important to state again that both approaches are biblical, and in reality most churches attempt to balance the 'head' and 'heart' approaches. It is right to emphasise biblical truth, as it is also right to emphasise communal worship and the personal reality of faith where people can praise God freely. Our purpose is not to criticise one or the other, or to state a preference for a 'head' or a 'heart' fellowship. A problem can occur, however, when churches become lop-sided and overly emphasise one or other of these areas at the expense of the other.

Danger points

1. Christians who have a strong emphasis on the *feeling* side of faith may have particular problems if feelings of anxiety or depression mean that they no longer sense the closeness of God or people in the fellowship. This loss of 'feeling' leaves them vulnerable to drifting away from God.
2. Christians who have a *thinking*-centred (intellectual) faith may have particular problems in their faith if they start to have doubts about their faith and find themselves unsure about what they believe.

3. Some sins are worse than others

You may have noticed that some sins are treated more seriously in church than others; they may be discussed in hushed tones in small groups, or roundly denounced in sermons or Bible study groups.

Task: Think about the attitudes you, other Christians or your church leaders have towards the following behaviours and consider how they are judged and emphasised within the church.

1. Pride.
2. Hypocrisy.
3. Stealing.
4. Lust.
5. Sex before marriage.
6. Prejudice against members or leaders from another Christian denomination.
7. Showing favouritism towards those who are more economically successful in life.

Q. Are any of these actions seen as 'worse' than others? If so, which?

Q. Would you be happier admitting to some of these behaviours/attitudes than to others?

Now that you have done this, think about what the Bible has to say about these actions and attitudes.

1. Pride (Proverbs 8:13).
2. Hypocrisy (1 Peter 2:1 – along with envy, malice, slander and deceit).
3. Stealing (Ephesians 4:28).
4. Lust (Colossians 3:5 – and also impurity and greed).
5. Sex before marriage (Colossians 3:5).
6. Prejudice against members or leaders from another Christian denomination (1 John 2:9–11).
7. Showing favouritism towards the successful in life (Leviticus 19:15).

While the consequences of some of these sins may be more destructive than others, it is clear that the Bible sees *all* of this behaviour as being equally wrong. As we saw above, the harshest words of Jesus tended to be reserved for those who considered themselves to be better than others and were guilty of pride and hypocrisy. Jesus was known as a friend of tax-collectors, who were generally thieves, and those who had fallen into sexual sin. It always seemed that these people were more responsive to the call of Jesus to turn from sin and to serve God; it was those who believed themselves to be righteous that had the hardest hearts. Yet in church society financial and sexual misdeeds are so often seen as the really serious crimes, and we are more prone to tolerate gossiping, pride and hypocrisy. It is often simply our own cultural values that make us feel worse about certain behaviour, and these values may be reinforced or fuelled by prejudice from within a local church or Christian community.

4. Thinking that we don't deserve good things

One problem that often occurs during times of anxiety and depression is that we can become so low and self-critical that we begin to believe that we don't deserve good things, and instead only deserve bad things. This may cause us to accept relentless verbal abuse from a spouse or partner because at the time we think that we are only receiving what we deserve. This can prevent us making changes in our lives that would really benefit how we feel.

TOWARDS OVERCOMING ANXIETY AND DEPRESSION

The following areas are known to play a part in the causes of anxiety and depression. Not every factor is present in every case. Because these factors can all play a part in the causes of anxiety and depression, they also can be targets for change in working to overcome these problems. You will find out about this in Part 3.

Situation, relationship and practical problems contributing to anxiety and depression

When someone faces a large number of problems they may begin to feel overwhelmed and distressed. Dwelling on the problems may worsen things still further and quickly get them out of proportion. These problems may include:

- Debts, housing or other difficulties.
- Problems in relationships with family, friends, fellow church members or colleagues, etc.
- Other difficult situations that you face.

You will find out about how to tackle practical problems in Chapter 7 of Part 3 of the book.

Psychological and spiritual aspects of anxiety and depression

For the Christian, anxiety and depression always has a spiritual dimension (as do all other aspects of life). Your faith may help support you through your distress. The next chapters will help you to find out how to achieve this through your own personal devotional life (Chapter 5) and within your own church (Chapter 8).

Physical factors contributing to anxiety and depression

Physical changes are a recognised part of significant anxiety and depression. Physical factors – such as a deficiency of chemicals in the brain known as 'amines' – occur in severe depression, and altered brain amine levels also occur in anxiety and panic.

These changes may also be caused by:

- Certain drugs or medications. These may lower amine levels in the brain and cause depression.
- Physical illnesses (e.g. anaemia, undiagnosed diabetes, hormone disorders and heart disease). These are among a range of physical illnesses that can cause depression. That is why it is important to have a proper physical examination and sometimes blood tests when you are stressed or depressed. If you have not had these, discuss whether they are needed with your health care practitioner.
- Excessive alcohol or the use of many illegal drugs. These may contribute to mood problems. Occasionally, some prescribed medications can cause low energy levels and depression or

anxiety-like symptoms. If your symptoms have begun or worsened after starting medication and you think this may be the case, please discuss this with your doctor.

What about genetics?

Studies show that in the family of someone with very severe depression, there is an increased risk that other relatives will also experience psychiatric disorders such as depression, or other problems such as alcohol abuse. Similar studies also suggest that genetics may explain some of the risk of experiencing anxiety and panic. However, just because a close relative has experienced anxiety or depression does not mean that this is the reason why you are feeling like this. It may be part of the reason, but in most cases other factors such as practical problems or psychological factors are also present. If one of your parents suffered from anxiety or depression while you were growing up, while there may be genetic factors involved it is also quite likely that there are elements of your upbringing that were affected as a result and may have added to the likelihood of you experiencing similar difficulties. You will find out about the different psychiatric treatments for anxiety and depression in Chapter 9. This also includes a description of the use of antidepressants and other medication as part of a treatment approach.

Learning from the past

Sometimes it can be helpful to think about how you have tried to deal with depression, worry and stress in the past, to see if this can help you to identify *effective ways* of dealing with your problems now. This can also help you to avoid repeating *unhelpful ways* of dealing with anxiety or depression that haven't worked before.

Q. How have I tried to deal with my worry/low mood in the past?

Have these attempts been *helpful* or *unhelpful*? Unhelpful ways might include over-eating, drinking too much alcohol, repeatedly asking for reassurance from others, or checking things again and again.

Write down any *helpful things* you have done here:

Now write down any *unhelpful things* you have done here:

Part 3 of this book will help you begin to learn new strategies to deal with anxiety and depression, and show you how to put these approaches into practice.

SUMMARY

The chapter has covered:

- The impact of unhelpful inner/core beliefs on anxiety and depression.
- The problem attitudes that are common among us as Christians and within our churches. You have thought about how these develop and about whether such attitudes are creating problems for you.
- The causes of anxiety and depression have been described, and you have had the opportunity to think about the ways you have tried to deal with these feelings in the past. This has helped you to begin to consider helpful and unhelpful ways you have used before to improve how you feel.

Putting into practice what you have learned
Pray the following prayer, then meditate on the Bible verses that follow.

CLOSING PRAYER

When you can, pray this prayer silently or preferably aloud.

Father, thank you for your unconditional love for me. When I look at myself, I am often critical and focus on my faults, and the problems they cause, but thank you that you don't see me or judge me in that way. Thank you that you look at me and see someone who is loved and forgiven. Thank you that in my relationship with you, grace always has the last word.

Sometimes it is really difficult for me to live life as a Christian – where temptations are great, and where bad things have happened to me and to those I care for. Thank you for the grace and mercy that made Jesus willing to die in my place so that I would not have to face the punishment for my wrong attitudes and behaviour. Sometimes though, Lord, I find it hard to fully accept this, and I ask that you will help me, and the other people reading this book, to trust that this is true. I want to place into your hands the problem situations that I face, and to ask that you will help me to change the problem attitudes that I have.

Father, please bring your healing and gentle change in how I see and judge myself and others. Let me see things with your eyes and hear things with your ears. Help me to begin to make changes in the focus of my thinking. Help me also to choose to dwell on helpful areas such as your love, mercy and grace. Finally, I pray that you will show me how to alter what I do so that I can re-establish a balanced life – one that helps me experience more of you and one that is a help to others.

Amen.

Bible meditation

Remind yourself of what the Bible says and focus on this when you notice any of your unhelpful thinking styles and unhelpful inner core beliefs.

- Read Romans 5, preferably all the way through, but if this is difficult concentrate on verses 1–5 and 15–21.
- Now read Psalm 103:1–5.

Think and pray about each of these passages. As you do so, try to answer the following questions:

- What is helpful for me in this passage?
- What do God's promises say to me at this time?
- How can I hold onto these promises and keep them in my heart?
- What would prevent me taking hold of these promises for myself? What can I ask God to do in me to prevent this happening?
- What changes can I make myself to ensure I choose to focus on what he has to say?

Write the most helpful verses out and carry them around with you so that you can remind yourself of their truth when you need to.

PART 3: OVERCOMING YOUR PROBLEMS

5

Maintaining your walk with God – practical things you can do that can make a difference

Problems such as anxiety and depression can cause particular problems for Christians. Chapters 2 to 4 will have helped you to find out more about the impact of anxiety and depression on you. Think about what you have learned from your reading of these chapters. The current chapter will help you to think about the impact of these changes on your relationship with God and focus on practical things you can do within your own devotional life to improve how you feel.

What are the main challenges that anxiety and depression cause to you as a Christian?

The different problem areas in anxiety and depression can be summarised using the Five Areas Assessment:

Altered feelings/emotions

Feeling low and unable to enjoy things are core symptoms of depression. Things that normally would be rewarding and provide a sense of fun/pleasure and achievement may have little or no emotional impact. Worry, stress, tension and panic may all occur when you are anxious. These can be accompanied by feelings of guilt, irritability and sometimes anger. Perhaps one of the most difficult emotions for us as Christians to experience is the feeling of being cut off and distanced from God. As you read the Bible, the 'life' in the passages may seem to have disappeared and your prayer life may become difficult, with little or no sense of God's presence. This isn't because God has gone away, but the depression affects how you feel. This experience is similar to the loss of emotions noticed in other areas of life too and is a normal part of depression.

Altered physical symptoms

You may have problems with low energy, poor concentration and disrupted sleep that together can make it difficult to read the Bible. You may find yourself reading the same verses again and again without them really seeming to go in. At church, you may find yourself distracted and put off by the bustle of children and others around you, or find that you don't have the energy to get out of the house to be there in the first place.

Altered thinking

If you are feeling anxious or depressed, you may have a very negative view of your own value and of how others see you. You may think that God has abandoned you, or is punishing you. You may start thinking back to past upsetting memories, or focusing on things that you have done wrong in an attempt to try to make sense of why you are feeling like this. Because we have our own expectations of how we *should/must/ought* to behave as Christians, you may feel under pressure to conform to a particular image that is deemed to be appropriate in your fellowship – wear a smile, hug lots of people and so on. You may not feel like singing, worshipping, praying, and certainly not listening to a sermon, and home may seem like a safe refuge to avoid all this pressure. You may begin to show a number of *unhelpful thinking styles*, with extreme and unhelpful thinking that worsens how you feel emotionally, and has an unhelpful impact on what you do.

Altered behaviour

Think about what you have *stopped doing* because of your anxiety and depression. It is common to reduce your activity levels. You may avoid doing things because it is harder to do things when you think you won't enjoy them, are scared by the idea of doing them, or quite simply lack the motivation and energy to do them. At times you will almost certainly feel like *avoiding going to church*, not because of a lack of belief but because of the need to interact with people while there. You may possibly be intimidated simply by going into places where there are a lot of other people and this may include church. You may also be tempted to stop going to mid-week Bible study groups, reading the Bible, or praying/talking to God because of these feelings. This reduced activity can backfire because it cuts you off from important sources of support from God, other members of your church and friends/relatives.

You may find yourself starting to develop a number of *unhelpful behaviours* such as drinking to block unpleasant emotions. These may make you feel better in the short term, but can worsen how you feel in the long term and further add to your problems. A vicious circle of unhelpful behaviour may result.

Situation, relationship or practical problems

These may include problems such as poor housing, debt, work or unemployment problems, unsupportive or violent/cruel relationships at home or elsewhere. Unfortunately, sometimes distress may be caused by things said or done within church by other Christians. When you are depressed, you may misinterpret what other people say, feel criticised and even 'got at'. You may find yourself facing a variety of difficult situations, all of which can sometimes seem too hard to overcome by yourself.

What can you do if you feel like this?

The following summarises some practical advice that can help you to maintain a helpful balance to your life when you are feeling anxious and depressed. These are truths that you can hold on to when you feel distressed. Hold on to them firmly, not because we suggest it, but because God tells you that they are true for you. A key thing to remember here is that you are not by yourself – you have the support of God and his Church to help you through this. This doesn't mean that all your problems will suddenly disappear, but it does mean that you will have someone there who will not abandon you.

Remember that God loves you as you are, not as you would like to be

It is important to remember that in God's eyes, however we feel about ourselves, we are still his children and of great importance to him. Furthermore, whatever we have done or failed to do God readily forgives us, and desires to restore us in our relationship with him. Thus our feelings of poor self-esteem and guilt at things we have done or have failed to do are just that – feelings – and more to do with the state of our mind than reality.

How do we know this?

'How great is the love the Father has lavished on us, that we should be called children of God! And that is what we are!' (1 John 3:1).

'This is how God showed his love among us: He sent his one and only Son into the world that we might live through him. This is love: not that we loved God, but that he loved us and sent His Son as an atoning sacrifice for our sins' (1 John 4:9–10).

Overcoming doubts

- Choose to dwell on God's word. Write down and carry around helpful verses that summarise God's love for you.
- Talk to trusted Christians about your fears and pray with them.
- Ask God to help you through these doubts and fears, and to return to you the feeling of his presence in your life. Thank him that even if you don't feel his presence, he is there.

Try to spend some time with the following questions. Don't feel pressurised into giving 'right' or 'correct' answers; try to be honest about how you are feeling right now, as well as remembering how real the love and care of God was before you felt like this.

Q. How is God's love working in me at the moment? (If you can't think of anything just now, keep thinking, or ask a friend who is a Christian who may be able to help you answer this question):

Q. When God reaches out to me and offers me support, how can I make sure that I am able to respond to his love?

Q. Imagine that Jesus is physically standing right next to you now. Try to imagine what he would say to you in your current situation. What words of support and encouragement would he offer, and how could you act on them?

SETTING REALISTIC SPIRITUAL GOALS

Reading the Bible and praying can be especially hard work when we feel depressed or anxious; these basic devotional exercises, however, are part of the solution and not part of the problem. What do we mean by this?

Talking to God can be very difficult when you are feeling distressed. As well as the poor motivation, concentration and energy already mentioned, you may also notice that it is difficult settling your mind, and that upsetting or negative thoughts and distressing memories intrude again and again. If you are someone who has high standards and expectations as a person, you may approach a time of prayer with a long list of things and people you *should* be praying for, and a belief that you *must* spend at least half an hour in God's presence, and that if you can only pray hard enough and long enough your distress will go away. The problem with these sorts of rules is that if five minutes later your mind has wandered a dozen times, and you are only on item three on your list, you may give up in despair and want to stop praying altogether. A different approach is therefore more likely to be helpful.

Two of the feelings that most frequently accompany anxiety and depression are guilt and a sense of failure. We may bring a sense of guilt upon ourselves by having unrealistic expectations of what we can do. Deciding that we will pray for half an hour or more each day, and read seven or eight chapters of the Bible, starting at Genesis and completing the whole Bible in six months, are almost certainly unhelpful targets. If you set unachievable goals this will be unhelpful for you and your relationship with God. The danger is that during times of anxiety and depression, you will find it increasingly difficult to achieve these targets. You may give up after the first few days and then become self-critical, feel guilty and judge yourself a failure. These thoughts come from yourself, not God.

The problem is that although having high targets for prayer and Bible reading may seem like a good idea – instead, for many it reflects personality traits and rules that we have learned over the years and were part of our make-up *even before* we became Christians. If the motivation to pray and read the Bible is because we should/must/ought/got to rather than to meet God and learn from him, the motives reflect our own self-imposed human values, rather than spiritual ones. Even if to begin with you achieve your target, the prayer and reading may become lifeless, because it misses the real purpose of prayer and Bible study.

Ask yourself the following questions:

Q. Do I set unrealistic targets in what I expect of myself?

In prayer?	Yes ❑	No ❑
In reading the Bible?	Yes ❑	No ❑
In going to church?	Yes ❑	No ❑
In what I do at home/work?	Yes ❑	No ❑
In other areas of my life?	Yes ❑	No ❑

The consequence of these high standards and black or white ways of seeing/judging things is that you may become so discouraged that you completely give up any prayer or reading *at all* and then go for several weeks without talking to God or reading any of the Bible. This is sad, because the truth is that Bible reading and prayer are the most reliable ways of communicating with God and hearing what he has to say to us.

Instead, a better approach is to set yourself realistic goals. Instead of an all-or-nothing approach, find a middle ground, where you may spend less time praying and reading the Bible but you still manage to do it at least to some extent even when you fell unwell.

CHOOSING REALISTIC GOALS IN YOUR PRAYER LIFE

Re-assess expectations during times of anxiety or depression

- Aim to pray for no more than five minutes to begin with. If this is easy for you, then slowly increase your prayer time if you wish to.
- Approach God *without* any lists that you *have* to complete. Ask him to show you what to pray. If you find it difficult finding the words, consider using a well-known prayer such as the Lord's prayer to begin with.

Use a structure to help you to pray

- A helpful way into prayer may be to use the words of a Bible passage that you have read, allowing your mind to explore the ideas and reflect on them. This may well lead you into other areas of prayer, including praise and worship, as well as bringing to your mind people you could pray for.
- Pray for others, perhaps the other readers of this book as they struggle with you to maintain their own relationship with God.
- Pray with others – but remember to keep it short. Having someone round to pray with you can be helpful, but you have to make the decision whether this is helpful or intrusive for you. When you pray with someone else, make sure *you* also pray – silently if need be. Their support and prayers are important, but you also have direct access to God.

- Remember, your mind will almost certainly wander quite a lot as you pray, and you will find yourself needing to jump back to speaking to God. Don't let this bother you; most of us have difficulties concentrating on prayer at the best of times, and having to return from distracting thoughts is quite normal and nothing to feel guilty about.
- When you think that you have prayed as much as you want then simply stop; there is nothing to stop you spending further time with God later in the day.

Ask the Holy Spirit to help

Paul tells us that when we don't know what to pray for, we should ask the Holy Spirit to show us what to pray for (Romans 8:26–7). This can be particularly helpful when we are at a loss about how to and what to pray for.

Check out what you learn

As you pray, particularly if you are reflecting on a passage from the Bible, you may sense God speaking to you in a particular way or about a particular aspect of your life, or your relationship with him.

- *Write down* anything you think God might be saying to you so that you can remember it and reflect on it later.
- It is a good idea to *share these thoughts* with another Christian you trust, so that they can help you understand what God may be saying to you.

If you have kept a prayer log or diary over the years, look back on it to remind yourself of how God has spoken to you in the past – focusing on his promises and your proven experience of him can be a great encouragement during more difficult times.

> **Key point:** If the things we sense God is saying to us are words of *condemnation* or convey condemnation, telling us we are useless and a failure, then these are not from God – instead this is caused by our own doubts, fears and negative thoughts, which are a normal part of depression and anxiety. While God may convict us of things in our lives that need to be put right, he will not condemn us or tell us that we are useless to him. God's final word to us is always one of grace and hope.

CHOOSING REALISTIC GOALS IN YOUR BIBLE READING

Reading the Bible is a helpful way of hearing what God has to say, reminding you of his promises of love and forgiveness, and of your hope for the future. As with prayer, the key is to:

- Have realistic and helpful expectations – set yourself achievable goals.
- Keep reading God's word if you can – even if it is only a verse a day.
- Read the Bible in small chunks, and focus on books that will help to meet your needs.
- Choose 'supportive' Bible topics.
- Not read an entire book.
- Allow yourself time with God to talk and reflect with him about what you have read.

Use a structure to help you to read the Bible

You may find it helpful to use *Bible reading notes*, of which there are a wide variety, to help you with your Bible reading. These notes come in a number of forms, and are generally of very good quality. The advantages of using them are that they can help you to understand the passage you are reading, and encourage the discipline of reading the Bible daily. They also have drawbacks, however. Since the choice of Bible passage is decided by the publisher or writer of the booklet it may or may not be helpful for you at this particular time. The thought of having to read not only a Bible passage but also some further material may also discourage you from opening your Bible in the first place. It is more important to read the Bible, even a few verses, on a regular basis than to grapple with someone else's comments if this feels too much to do. In short if you find that Bible reading notes help you, then use them, but feel able to lay them aside if they are not helping you at the moment.

Plan your reading

The psalms are very important, because they express a wide range of feelings, from elation to despair, from joy to sadness at sin. They reflect the characteristics of God in language full of beauty and awe, and they reflect on our relationship with the creator of the universe. They are full of praise and are very human, even when the writer feels an underlying sense of anxiety or failure. Furthermore, with a few exceptions, notably Psalm 119, they are generally short, and are ideal to read in two or three minutes at a nice slow pace, following which you can spend a few minutes simply reflecting on what you have read.

You may find that some of the following psalms help you in this:

- Psalm 4: God's protection and peace.
- Psalm 8: The greatness of God.
- Psalm 13: Praying for relief from despair.
- Psalm 46: God's security.
- Psalm 51: God's forgiveness and cleansing of sin.
- Psalm 139: God is always with us and knows us intimately.

Other books to focus on are the Gospels, Acts and perhaps some of the shorter letters in the New Testament. Aim to read a paragraph at a time, rather than a whole chapter, allowing the words and thoughts to sink in, and then reflect on what these things mean in your own life.

When reading the passages, ask yourself:

- What does this say about God?
- What do God's promises say to me at this time?
- What does this say about my own anxiety/depression?
- What is God wanting me to learn through what is happening?
- How can I hold on to these promises and keep them in my heart? What would prevent me taking hold of these promises for myself?
- How can I put what I am learning into practice in a helpful way, that is realistic, based on how I feel now?

What not to read

There are some books that are probably best avoided when your mood is low. While all the books in the Bible have important teaching in them, some may also make you feel worse at the moment because of the subjects they deal with. Lengthy Old Testament passages addressing matters such as requirements for animal sacrifice and ceremonial cleanliness are important, but probably not the sort of reading that will help you if you are feeling depressed.

GOING TO CHURCH – MAINTAINING A BALANCE

Although it may be tempting at times to start missing church services if you are feeling very anxious or depressed, it is almost always better to go unless your feelings of depression and anxiety are made worse by attending church. You will find out more about this in Chapter 8 when you will look at your relationship with your church fellowship.

Speaking about the problem

This can be useful but is often avoided by the sufferer and by churches. It is often not easy to speak about the fact that you have depression or anxiety. This is especially true if you are uncertain about what is the matter with you. To speak about the problem is to admit that you may be unwell. To tell another person is potentially risky since you may not know how they will react or how they will treat you afterwards. Most of this concern is unfounded since in the vast majority of cases, you will find that you receive a helpful and supportive response.

Dealing with particular problems in your devotional life

Dealing with a loss of feelings

When it comes to our individual relationship with God, we may have to accept that to some extent it will be hard work if we are experiencing emotional distress. Our feelings about God are likely to reflect our mood level, and there may be times when for long periods God seems remote. So how can we maintain our walk with God when we are in such a position?

First we need to recognise that feelings are not all-important, and understand that however we feel about God, he has not abandoned us. Truth does not change according to how we feel at any given time, and facts remain facts even when we struggle to grasp them. So the reality of God's love and compassion for us does not alter according to the state of our mental health; it is only the way we feel about it that is different.

Second we will not always feel as we do now. One of the most difficult elements of depression or anxiety is the feeling that we are in a deep dark tunnel, struggling to make progress; not only can we see no light at the end, but we also find it difficult to believe that we ever will. Although it may be difficult to hold on to faith at these times, try to keep reminding yourself that a return to good mental health will almost certainly bring with it a fresh realisation not only of God's presence in your life, but also an understanding that he was in reality always there. No matter how you feel about the apparent absence of God, it will not always be like this.

Is my problem due to spiritual warfare?

Christians are always involved in spiritual warfare. Because anxiety and depression affect our relationship with God, as well as our views of ourselves, they have an impact on our spiritual life. Both anxiety and depression can lead us to feel cut off from God, guilty, bad and unloved. These are normal consequences of these distressing disorders, and are not symptoms of demonic attack.

Unfortunately there are many misunderstandings about the nature of mental illness in general, and depression in particular, within the Church, and a number of inaccurate and unhelpful attitudes persist. Some common misunderstandings and wrong ideas/rules are:

- Since Christians have the joy of the Lord they should never feel depressed or anxious.
- Depression is always the result of demonic activity and you need deliverance ministry.
- Depression is the consequence of a curse, or the sinful actions of you or your ancestors.
- If others have prayed for healing then you only need to have enough faith and you will be healed. If you are not healed then this is your fault.
- Depression means that you are not committed enough to God, and if you were doing more for him you would not be suffering as you are.

These unhelpful 'rules' may be held by others in the church you go to, or you yourself may believe them to be true.

There are a number of difficulties with seeing anxiety or depression as having *primarily* a spiritual cause.

- We completely agree that there are always spiritual aspects to anxiety and depression (as there are in everything in life for a Christian). However, we see these as being a secondary consequence of the emotional distress that is part of these illnesses. Strong claims that all anxiety and depression is spiritual in origin are unhelpful because they miss the point that the actual problem is anxiety and depression.
- Those offering these sorts of 'solutions' may have little understanding of what it is like to experience depression or anxiety, or about the normal consequences of the problems. The danger is that the problems can actually be worsened by conversations with people who hold these views.
- Most importantly, the unhelpful prayer and focus on spiritual attack can backfire by creating more feelings of guilt and an even greater sense of failure. They also commonly prevent the person from dealing with the actual problem – their anxiety, depression and longer-term difficulties such as low self-esteem.

What to do if a Christian friend/leader is concerned that the problem is *primarily* a spiritual one

- Talk to your doctor or someone who knows about mental health problems, and see to what extent your problems 'fit' the sorts of symptoms that make up anxiety and depression. Chapters 2 and 3 can also help you with this.
- If someone tries to tell you that your emotional distress is a spiritual problem, acknowledge that the anxiety and depression has had an impact on you spiritually – perhaps that it is harder to pray or read the Bible etc. – but say that this is a *consequence* of your low energy, poor concentration, not being able to sleep and other symptoms that are a part of your illness. Ask them to pray with you about these difficulties, and perhaps ask them for help in supporting you through this.
- If another Christian tells you that you should stop taking prescribed medication such as antidepressants, or that taking them is evidence of a lack of faith in God's ability to heal, they unfor-

tunately know little about mental health problems or their treatment. Gently suggest that they perhaps need to learn something more about them. Ask if they would say the same thing if their own parent/spouse or they themselves had broken a leg or had a heart attack. Tell them that you see the tablets as being only part of the solution, and that prayer and pastoral support from other Christians is very important to you in getting better. Don't stop taking prescribed medication without a discussion with your doctor. The person is most likely offering this advice 'in love', so thank them again for the support, tell them that you disagree about what they say about the tablets, but that you would really value their prayer support.

- Educate them – they may not know much about anxiety and depression. Tell them what you have learned from this book about mental health problems. Ask them to read this or other books (but don't lend them your copy if you are still reading it!). They may particularly find Part 4 of the book helpful to read, and also Chapter 9, which covers the role of different treatments including antidepressant treatments.
- If anyone continues to tell you that they suspect that there is primarily a spiritual cause for your emotional problems (such as your or others' sin, or a direct spiritual attack on you), ask them why they say this. What evidence do they have for these concerns? Is it in accord with God's word? Is what they are saying offered in love? Is what they say supported by the judgment of others who are spiritually mature and whose advice you respect?
- Seek advice from several people who have spiritual discernment and common sense. Don't accept that the problem is primarily a spiritual one until you are happy that a number of committed Christians who have knowledge of *both* mental and spiritual problems all say the same thing, and all your questions have been properly answered.

SUMMARY

The chapter has covered:

- The possible impact of anxiety and depression on your personal devotional life.
- The unhelpful impact that having high standards and attitudes can have on you, and how this can actually harm your relationship with God.
- Practical things you can do to maintain your prayer and Bible reading by setting yourself realistic targets, and allowing God to speak to you through your personal devotional times.
- A discussion of what you can do if you have lost your feeling of God's presence, or if others are telling you that the cause of your problems is primarily a spiritual one.

Putting into practice what you have learned
The important thing is to think about how you can put what you have learned into practice. One way is by praying this prayer and then completing the following tasks over the next week or so.

CLOSING PRAYER

When you can, pray this prayer silently or preferably aloud.

Dear Father, thank you for being here, for listening to me and for loving me. Thank you that no matter how I feel, you are here and promise to be with me. Thank you for all that I've learned in this chapter.

Lord, sometimes it is hard to stay close to you, to feel your presence or appreciate your love. Sometimes it's hard to spend time with you, to speak to you, to listen to you, to read your word and spend time with Christian friends. Help me to overcome how I feel and to move on from these feelings of depression and anxiety.

Lord, I commit myself to you. I commit myself to spending a few minutes with you each day. Give me the help and encouragement to do this. Give me as well a thirst for your word. As I come to it, speak to me and help me to understand it even if it is just a short passage I read.

Lord, I think about church and friends there. I thank you that they care. Help me to share with them the difficult times, to spend time with them and to pray with them. Give me the strength to worship in church, to be with others Sunday by Sunday. Take away the worries that I have about this and let me rely on you being there with me.

I also pray for those other people who are currently reading this book, who are feeling cut off or distanced from you. Let them also know your touch and your presence. Help them to keep praying and reading your word, and please, Lord, give them support and encouragement as they do this.

Lord, be with us now.

Amen.

Bible meditation

Remind yourself of what the Bible says about your relationship with God.

- Read Psalm 23 a verse at a time. Think about each verse. Where the passage says 'me' or 'I', read your own name. The Lord is your Shepherd and he will restore you.
- Read Philippians 4:4–7. It is difficult to rejoice if you feel down and anxious but try to thank God for his love and care for you. Remember God is present and will listen to you.

Suggested points for action

- Reread this chapter to spend time thinking about your own response to anxiety and depression.
- Think about ways of maintaining your own prayer and Bible reading. How can you meet God through these and continue to hear from him?
- Think about any high standards that you have, that may be adding to your problems. How can you choose to act against these, and seek a more balanced approach to what you do – one that is helpful for you and your relationship with God?

If you have any difficulties with these tasks, don't worry. Just do what you can.

My notes

6

Identifying and changing unhelpful thinking

This chapter provides an introduction to some of the techniques used in Cognitive Behaviour Therapy (CBT). But first, what do we mean by the term 'Cognitive Behaviour Therapy'?

What is Cognitive Behaviour Therapy?

Cognitive means thinking, and Cognitive Behaviour Therapy describes a type of treatment that aims to help you to identify and change the unhelpful thinking styles and behaviours that are often a part of anxiety and depression. CBT has a proven effectiveness in treating these problems. It can help you in getting better and can work alongside your Christian faith. CBT is usually offered as weekly or fortnightly sessions with a qualified or accredited CBT practitioner on an individual basis, or within a treatment group. CBT treatments are also commonly accessed by using structured self-help materials – for example, this book.

The main advantages of CBT are that it:

- Provides a clear model that can help you to understand your problems and identify targets for change – the Five Areas Model.
- Focuses on helping you to overcome these difficulties.

In Part 2 of this book, you have already identified many of the problems you are experiencing in each of the five areas:

1. The different situations, relationships and practical problems you face – including the impact of your problems on your relationship with God and with other people in your local church.
2. Altered thinking with extreme and unhelpful thinking styles.
3. Altered feelings (such as feeling low, anxious or angry).
4. Altered physical symptoms (such as not sleeping or having low energy levels).
5. Altered behaviour (with reduced activity or unhelpful behaviours such as drinking to excess).

The CBT approach works by aiming to provide you with key information to help you to understand the impact of anxiety and depression on you. It also aims to help you to improve how you feel by teaching you new skills to deal with your unhelpful thoughts and altered behaviour. It does this by *asking you questions* so that you can find out important information about your problems for yourself. Answering the questions in this book can help you to apply what you are learning to your own life.

This chapter builds upon what you have learned already by providing a detailed description of some useful new skills for identifying and challenging unhelpful and extreme thoughts. The key is to make changes one step at a time – with each step building upon previous steps to bring about helpful changes in how you feel, what you think and what you do. By practising each step during the week, you will be able to build your skills in overcoming anxiety and depression.

What is the first step?
To begin with we want to encourage you to start thinking about:

- Short-term targets: changes you can make today, tomorrow and next week.
- Medium-term targets: changes to be put into place over the next few weeks and months.
- Longer-term targets: where you want to be in six months or a year.

This chapter will focus on helping you to change unhelpful and extreme thinking. Chapter 7 will help you to learn skills in practical problem solving, and look at how you can use these principles to overcome problems of reduced activity and unhelpful behaviour. First, let's think together about the sort of altered thinking that occurs during times of anxiety and depression.

Revision

Unhelpful thinking styles
In order to be able to challenge and change unhelpful and extreme thinking styles, it is important first of all to be aware of the common changes in thinking that can occur as part of anxiety and depression. This was summarised in Chapters 2 and 3. Anxiety and depression can lead to one or more of the following unhelpful thinking styles:

Unhelpful thinking style	Typical negative thoughts
1. Bias against myself	I overlook my strengths. I focus on my weaknesses. I downplay my achievements. I am my own worst critic.
2. Putting a negative slant on things (negative mental filter)	I see things through dark tinted glasses. I tend to focus on the negative in situations.

Unhelpful thinking style	Typical negative thoughts
3. Having a gloomy view of the future (make negative predictions/jump to the worst conclusion – catastrophising)	I make negative predictions about the future. I predict that things will go wrong. I predict that the very worst events will happen.
4. Negative view about how others see me (mind-reading)	I mind-read what others think of me. I often think that others don't like me/think badly of me.
5. Bearing all responsibility	I take the blame if things go wrong. I feel responsible for whether everyone else has a good time. I take unfair responsibility for things that are not my fault.
6. Making extreme statements/rules	I use the words 'always', 'never' and 'typical' a lot to summarise things. I make myself a lot of 'must', 'should' 'ought' or 'got to' rules.

All of these unhelpful thinking styles are examples of extreme thinking.

Why is extreme thinking so unhelpful?
Because these thoughts are so biased and extreme, they are almost always untrue – and against what God says is true about a situation. They therefore become part of the problem and are unhelpful to us in all areas of our lives. Typically, when these sorts of unhelpful thoughts occur:

- *Your mood drops*: you may feel more depressed, upset, anxious, stressed or angry.
- *Your behaviour alters unhelpfully*: by either reducing what you do (avoidance or reduced activity) or leading you to start doing unhelpful things such as drinking too much to block how you feel.

These changes lead to the Vicious Circle of Reduced Activity or the Vicious Circle of Unhelpful Behaviours that were described in Chapter 3. You will find out how to overcome these problems in Chapter 7.

NOTICING UNHELPFUL THINKING STYLES: COMPLETING A THOUGHT INVESTIGATION WORKSHEET

In order to identify extreme or unhelpful thinking, try to watch for times when your mood suddenly changes (e.g. you feel sadder, or more anxious, upset or angry). Then ask, 'What went through my mind then?' Beginning to notice your unhelpful thinking styles is the first step for change, because when you start to notice these thoughts – the sort of thoughts that worsen how you feel and unhelpfully affect what you do – then you can begin to challenge them and improve how you feel.

A Five Areas Assessment can be used to help you to identify which unhelpful thinking styles you are prone to when you feel worse. The Thought Investigation Worksheet on pages 276–7 is to help you to 'play detective' and work at identifying the unhelpful thoughts that were present at the time when your mood dropped.

Remember that thoughts can include memories of the past, comments on the present, predictions about the future and also images/mental pictures.

Images/mental pictures in anxiety and depression

Some people (although not everyone) notice mental pictures or images in their minds when they feel very anxious, panicky or depressed. Images are a form of thought and like other thoughts can be very gloomy or scary. These may occur as 'still' images (like a photograph), or seem to be moving (like a video). Sometimes images may be in black and white or they can be in full colour. These may include the person having pictures of them collapsing or fainting, having a stroke or heart attack, going mad or being ridiculed or humiliated or losing control in front of others. As with all such thoughts, these images add to feelings of fear and/or depression and may lead the person unhelpfully to alter what they do; for example, in times of panic the person may suddenly stop what they are doing and hurry away.

Using the Thought Investigation Worksheet

The Thought Investigation Worksheet has been created to help guide you in the skill of how to identify extreme and unhelpful thoughts.

Task

Look at the Thought Investigation Worksheet that has been completed by Anne on pages 134–5. Anne has been feeling more depressed for the last few months. The worksheet summarises what happened to her when she was in church listening to the minister's talk.

As you read what she has put, remember that the purpose here is for Anne to carry out a Five Areas Assessment of what happened at the *specific* time when her mood altered. It is not aiming to summarise the full range of Anne's problems over several days or weeks. Instead it summarises what happened to her at 10.45 a.m. on Sunday, while she was sitting in church next to her friend Mary when the minister said, 'We must all try our very best to fulfil the roles that God calls us to.'

Her Thought Investigation Worksheet helps Anne to identify several thoughts showing different unhelpful thinking styles, and to begin to assess the impact on her of believing these. Here, she notices that she has several immediate negative thoughts:

1. 'I can't lead the group – people won't grow as they should.'
2. 'Look at what's happened with John. I really let him down.'
3. 'I am unusable by God.'

Anne identifies that the most upsetting/emotionally strongest immediate thought (sometimes called the 'hottest' thought because of the impact this has emotionally) is: 'I can't lead the group – people won't grow as they should', and she believed this 90 per cent at the time. This thought shows several unhelpful thinking styles and had an unhelpful impact on how she felt and what she did. Importantly she has identified an extreme thought (one that shows one of the unhelpful thinking styles) and also an unhelpful one – these are the target thoughts for change in CBT.

My own thought investigation

The Thought Investigation Worksheet has been designed to help you to analyse a specific time when your mood worsened and uses the Five Areas Assessment structure to help you to identify which extreme and unhelpful thoughts were present at that time. It uses the CBT approach of asking questions to help you to identify and then consider the impact of your immediate thoughts on how you felt and what you did.

Task: First, try to really think yourself back into a situation when your mood unhelpfully altered (for example a time when you felt more depressed, weepy, anxious, stressed, panicky, angry or irritable). Choose a time that is *fairly recent* so that you have a good memory of what happened. Now, complete the blank Thought Investigation Worksheet that is printed on pages 276–7. As you do so, summarise a *specific* time when you felt worse emotionally. Answer the questions in sequence working your way across from Columns 1 to 5. As you read the questions at the top of each column, really try to *slow down* how quickly you answer each question so that you are as accurate as you can be in your thought investigation. *Stop, think and reflect* as you consider the five different areas that can be affected when your mood altered. It can be tempting sometimes to skim-read the questions. Try not to do this because the questions have been carefully sequenced to help you to find out more about the different changes that occur during anxiety and depression.

Example of Anne completing her Thought Investigation Worksheet: Identifying extreme and unhelpful thinking

1. Situation/ relationship or practical problem when your mood unhelpfully altered	2. Altered emotional and physical feelings	3. What immediate thoughts are present at the time?
Think in detail: Where am I, what am I doing? Consider: • The time: What time of day is it? • The place: Where am I? • The people: Who is present? Who am I with? • The events: What has been said/What events happened?	Am I: • Low or sad? Guilty? • Worried, tense, anxious or panicky? • Angry or irritable? • Ashamed? a. State the feelings clearly. Try to be as precise as possible. If more than one feeling occurs, underline the most powerful feeling. b. How powerful is this feeling? (0-100%) c. Note down any strong physical sensations you notice.	What is going through my mind? How do I see: • Myself, my relationship with God, how others see me? • The current events/situation? • What might happen in the future? • My own body, behaviour or performance? • Any memories/images? a. State the thought(s) clearly. Try to be as precise as possible. If more than one thought occurs, underline the most powerful thought. b. Rate how strongly you believe the most powerful thought at the time (0–100%)
My situation: 10.45 a.m. on Sunday. Sitting in church next to my friend Mary. The minister has just said, 'We must all try our very best to fulfil the roles that God calls us to.'	**a. My feelings:** Feel low. Very guilty. **b. Powerfulness:** 90% guilty. **c. Physical sensations:** I had very low energy and felt quite tensed up in my neck.	**a. My immediate thoughts:** I can't lead the group – people won't grow as they should do. Look at what's happened with John, I really let him down. I am unusable by God. **b. Rating of belief in the most powerful thought at the time:** 0% 100% |-------------------------X------|

4. What unhelpful thinking style(s) occur?	5. Impact of the immediate thought(s)
1. Bias against myself. 2. Putting a negative slant on things (Negative mental filter). 3. Having a gloomy view of the future/jumping to the worst conclusion/catastrophic thinking. 4 Negative views about how others see me (Mind-reading). 5. Bearing all responsibility. 6. Making extreme statements/rules e.g. using 'must', 'should', 'ought', 'always', 'got to', 'typical' and 'never' statements. If any of the styles are present, you have identified an *extreme* thought.	a. What did I do differently? Consider any: • Reduced activity. • Unhelpful behaviours. b. What was the impact on: • Myself? • My relationship with God? • My view of others? • How I felt? • What I said? • What I did? • Overall, was the impact helpful or unhelpful? If there is an unhelpful impact, you have identified an *unhelpful* thought.
Thinking styles present: No(s): 1, 3, 5	**a. What I did differently:** I went home and cried. I phoned my minister and said that I am resigning from leading the group. **b. Overall, is it helpful or unhelpful for me to believe the thought?** Helpful Unhelpful ✓ I became upset and ended up pulling out completely from leading the group. I don't really think that is what God wanted me to do.

At first you may find it quite difficult to notice your own extreme and unhelpful thoughts. Try to complete your own Thought Investigation Worksheet at least once each day for the next few days to practise this skill. Always choose times when your mood has unhelpfully changed. Carrying out this sort of thought investigation can help you to practise how to do this so that over time you find that this task becomes easier. The best way of becoming aware of your extreme and unhelpful thinking is to begin to try to notice times when your mood unhelpfully alters (e.g. at times when you feel upset), and then to ask 'What is going through my mind right now?'

Key points:

- Noticing changes in your mood can be a helpful way of identifying your extreme and unhelpful thinking.
- If a thought shows one or more of the unhelpful thinking styles, and has an unhelpful impact on how you feel or what you do, then you have identified an example of an extreme and unhelpful thought. These are the sorts of thoughts that are identified in Columns 4 and 5 of your Thought Investigation Worksheet and which will be the focus for change.

The next step – the Thought Challenge Worksheet

Once you have become skilled at noticing and recording unhelpful and extreme thoughts, you are ready to move on to the next stage – how to challenge these thoughts. To do this, a second worksheet has been created – the Thought Challenge Worksheet. Together, these two worksheets allow you to identify and then challenge unhelpful and extreme thoughts.

- On pages 276–7 is the Thought Investigation Worksheet to help you to identify extreme and unhelpful thoughts.
- On pages 278–9 is the Thought Challenge Worksheet. This consists of a series of questions to help you complete the thought challenge process.

The Thought Challenge Worksheet follows on from the Thought Investigation Worksheet you have already completed and contains a number of extra columns of questions that will help you to challenge your own extreme and unhelpful thoughts.

- Use the questions at the top of each column to guide you through the process of challenging your extreme and unhelpful thoughts. The questions should each be read in turn and answered in the space provided on the worksheet.
- *Stop, think and reflect* as you answer each question.
- Write down your answers on the sheet of paper so that you can see them written down. This process of interacting with the materials, and seeing what you have written, will help you to question your negative thoughts.

You now have a chance to see a completed Thought Challenge Worksheet. Read Anne's completed worksheet on pages 138–9, which summarises the process of challenging her thought, 'I can't lead the group – people won't grow as they should', that she had previously identified using her own Thought Investigation Worksheet.

USING THE THOUGHT CHALLENGE WORKSHEET

The suggestions below and on page 140 will help you to get the most out of completing your own Thought Challenge Worksheet:

- Only challenge one thought at a time – this should be the thought that was underlined on your own Thought Investigation Worksheet. To begin with, try to avoid challenging thoughts

Anne's Thought Challenge Worksheet: Challenging the thought 'I can't lead the group – people

6. Reasons supporting the immediate thought	7. Reasons against the immediate thought
List all the reasons why I believed the immediate thought at the time.	Answer the following questions: • What would Jesus/God say to me about how he sees this thought? How would he encourage me? • Are there any other ways of explaining the situation that are more accurate? Is there anything to make me think the thought is incorrect? • If I wasn't feeling anxious/depressed, what would I say? • What would I tell a Christian friend who said the same thing? • What helpful things would other people say to me about it? • Have I heard *different opinions* from others about the thought?
My evidence supporting the immediate thought: • I have been feeling cut off from God for several months. It's difficult to hear his voice. • John has missed the last two study group meetings, and he seems to be trying to avoid me – he broke off our conversation quite quickly. • I just don't feel like I'm being effective. There was that large gap when no-one prayed at the start of the last meeting.	**My evidence against the immediate thought:** • God would tell me, 'You may feel cut off from me, but you aren't. I love you, – talk to me and to others about how you feel and I will support you.' • Everyone else has been coming to the group. People seem to enjoy it – there have been some really good times when we have learned a lot together and really supported each other. • If I wasn't feeling like this, I'd say there are lots of things that are going well in the group. • I'd tell a Christian friend, 'Keep praying, tell others and let the group support you.' • If I asked others in the group, I think they'd say that they appreciate coming. Mary said she really enjoyed last week's meeting.

won't grow as they should'

8. Come to a balanced conclusion	9. My plan for putting the balanced conclusion into practice
Use the answers from Columns 6 and 7 to try to come up with a *balanced, truthful* and *helpful* conclusion. Look for a *balanced conclusion* that you can believe. This should be based on *all* the information you have available to you and bear in mind the reasons for and against believing the immediate thought.	• How can I change what I do to reinforce my balanced conclusion? • How can I undermine my immediate negative thought by acting against it?
My balanced conclusion: I'm feeling low and this is affecting how I am thinking about the group. God loves me, and the others in the group also love and support me. I need to tell them how I feel, not completely give up the leadership. I also need to ask John why he has missed the last few meetings. **a. Rating of my belief in the balanced conclusion:** 0% 100% |---------------------------X---| **b. Re-rating of my belief in the immediate thought:** 0% 100% |---X---------------------------|	**My plan to put the balanced conclusion into practice:** 1. I won't resign – instead I'll speak to my minister and the group and say how I am feeling – that it feels as though I am doing too much, and at the moment my confidence is low. I'll ask if they can pray for me. 2. I am going to be realistic – although I'm not going to resign, I need to do less. I'll ask if I could lead the group just once a month, and ask if we could share out what we do for the next few months until I feel better. 3. Ask John if he is upset with me – and if that is why he missed the meetings. It's best to check this out directly rather than dwell on it all the time.

that begin 'I am . . .' or 'People are . . .' or 'The world is . . .' because core beliefs/rules like these are more difficult to challenge at first (see Chapter 4).

- The column that you are likely to have the *least difficulty* with is Column 6 – where you are asked to identify evidence *supporting* your extreme and unhelpful thought. People who are anxious and depressed are often very good at identifying reasons why things may go wrong, etc.
- The column that you are likely to have the *most difficulty* with is Column 7 – where you are asked to identify evidence *against* your extreme and unhelpful thought. Use the questions at the top of that column to help you in your answers.
- A crucial part of this process is putting your balanced conclusion into practice. This will help you to make important changes in your life, and avoid this task being a purely intellectual activity.

Putting the balanced conclusion into practice

One helpful approach to find out whether the new balanced conclusion is true and helpful is to *set up a test* to see if it is true in practice. One powerful action to test the helpfulness and accuracy of your own balanced conclusion is to *act on the balanced conclusion*, believing it to be true, and see what happens. This may mean choosing to do the *reverse* of what the immediate thought may be telling you.

Example

You are asked to friends for a meal. Your initial reaction is to say no as a result of an immediate thought, 'I won't enjoy it and I won't have anything to say.' Try to act against this thought (by going to the meal) in order to test out whether it is true. You may well find that the meal and the conversation go far better than you predicted and that you do enjoy it at least a little.

Important point
By far the best evidence for or against a negative thought is found through looking at the consequences of what happens when you choose to act or not act on it. *Reinforce* your balanced conclusions by acting on them. *Undermine* your extreme and unhelpful thoughts by acting against them.

Using the Thought Challenge Worksheet in anxiety and panic

In the example where Anne completed her own Thought Investigation and Thought Challenge Worksheets, she looked at a thought that is more likely to occur when someone is depressed and very self-critical. Let's now think in more detail about a different thought – one that can occur in extreme anxiety such as during a panic attack.

Example: a Five Areas Assessment of a panic attack
Mark is a 25-year-old man who has been experiencing panic attacks for the last three months. Whenever he goes shopping to a large supermarket he begins to feel anxious, and then begins to panic. This has led him to begin to avoid going to large shops. He is now going only to smaller local shops, and goes only when he predicts they will be quiet. Read through Mark's Thought Investigation Worksheet on pages 142–3.

As you read through what Mark has noticed, remember that the purpose here is for him to carry out a Five Areas Assessment of what happened at the specific time when his mood altered. It is not aiming to summarise the full range of his problems over several days or weeks. Instead it summarises what happened to him at 11 a.m. on Monday, when he was by himself in the crowded shop, buying some more bread.

Mark goes on to complete a Thought Challenge Worksheet in order to challenge his thought, 'I will faint.' Read what he has written there, and try to link his answers to the different questions in the columns of the worksheet.

Example of Mark completing his Thought Investigation Worksheet: Identifying extreme and unhelpful thinking

1. Situation/ relationship or practical problem when your mood unhelpfully altered	2. Altered emotional and physical feelings	3. What immediate thoughts are present at the time?
Think in detail: Where am I, what am I doing? Consider: • The time: What time of day is it? • The place: Where am I? • The people: Who is present? Who am I with? • The events: What has been said/What events happened?	Am I: • Low or sad?Guilty? • Worried, tense, anxious or panicky? • Angry or irritable? • Ashamed? a. State the feelings clearly. Try to be as precise as possible. If more than one feeling occurs, underline the most powerful feeling. b. How powerful is this feeling? (0-100%) c. Note down any strong physical sensations you notice.	What is going through my mind? How do I see: • Myself, my relationship with God, how others see me? • The current events/situation? • What might happen in the future? • My own body, behaviour or performance? • Any memories/images? a. State the thought(s) clearly. Try to be as precise as possible. If more than one thought occurs, underline the most powerful thought. b. Rate how strongly you believe the most powerful thought at the time (0–100%)
My situation: Monday at 11 a.m. By myself, going into the local shop to buy some bread, shop crowded.	**a. My feelings:** Very anxious. Panicky. **b. Powerfulness:** 85% anxious. **c. Physical sensations:** Tense, overbreathing, rapid heart, dry mouth, blurred vision, dizzy.	**a. My immediate thoughts:** I will faint. Images of myself on the floor passed out/unconscious. Everyone will be looking at me. **b. Rating of belief in the most powerful thought at the time:** 0% 100% |-------------------------X------|

during his panic attack

4. What unhelpful thinking style(s) occur?	5. Impact of the immediate thought(s)
1. Bias against myself. 2. Putting a negative slant on things (Negative mental filter). 3. Having a gloomy view of the future/jumping to the worst conclusion/catastrophic thinking. 4. Negative views about how others see me (Mind-reading). 5. Bearing all responsibility. 6. Making extreme statements/rules e.g. using 'must', 'should', 'ought', 'always', 'got to', 'typical' and 'never' statements. If any of the styles are present, you have identified an *extreme* thought.	a. What did I do differently? Consider any: • Reduced activity. • Unhelpful behaviours. b. What was the impact on: • Myself? • My relationship with God? • My view of others? • How I felt? • What I said? • What I did? • Overall, was the impact helpful or unhelpful? If there is an unhelpful impact, you have identified an *unhelpful* thought.
Thinking styles present: No(s): 1, 3	**a. What I did differently:** Avoidance – left the shop running and dropped the basket. **b. Overall, is it helpful or unhelpful for me to believe the thought?** Helpful Unhelpful ✓ This was unhelpful as it drew attention to me and reduced my confidence. I didn't really trust God to get me through it.

Mark's Thought Challenge Worksheet: Challenging the thought 'I will faint'

6. Reasons supporting the immediate thought	7. Reasons against the immediate thought
List all the reasons why I believed the immediate thought at the time.	Answer the following questions. • What would Jesus/God say to me about how he sees this thought? How would he encourage me? • Are there any other ways of explaining the situation that are more accurate? Is there anything to make me think the thought is incorrect? • If I wasn't feeling anxious/depressed, what would I say? • What would I tell a Christian friend who said the same thing? • What helpful things would other people say to me about it? • Have I heard *different opinions* from others about the thought?
My evidence supporting the immediate thought: • I was hot and sweaty and dizzy. The dizziness made me think I would collapse. • I couldn't catch my breath. • I felt really physically bad. • I was sure I would collapse.	**My evidence against the immediate thought:** • God would say, 'I am with you, even when you are weak, I will hold you up. Do not worry about anything.' • Well, I didn't collapse and I never have collapsed in spite of having had these fears for so long. That makes it pretty unlikely. • The book says that anxiety can create all of these same symptoms – and that overbreathing can cause dizziness. • This is all due to the anxiety – it's to do with tension and panic – not a physical problem. • I'd tell a friend, 'You've got to get that anxiety and overbreathing sorted out – that's the main problem.' • They'd say, 'You can overcome this – keep working on it with your doctor.' • My doctor said that it's impossible to collapse during panic because my heart is speeded up then and that is very different from what happens in a faint – where the heart slows down. Mine was definitely speeded up so I can't faint. He also says that to overcome overbreathing I should close my mouth and breathe through my nose, taking normal-sized breaths at a normal speed.

8. Come to a balanced conclusion	9. My plan for putting the balanced conclusion into practice
Use the answers from Columns 6 and 7 to try to come up with a *balanced, truthful* and *helpful* conclusion. Look for a *balanced conclusion* that you can believe. This should be based on *all* the information you have available to you and bear in mind the reasons for and against believing the immediate thought.	• How can I change what I do to reinforce my balanced conclusion? • How can I undermine my immediate negative thought by acting against it?
My balanced conclusion: I'm not going to collapse. The physical sensations are because of panic and over-breathing. I feel dizzy because of this. **a. Rating of my belief in the balanced conclusion:** 0% 100% |---------------------------X---| **b. Re-rating of my belief in the immediate thought:** 0% 100% |---X---------------------------|	**My plan to put the balanced conclusion into practice:** 1. I'll go back to the shop and use the Thought Identification and Challenge Worksheets **before** I go into the shop so that I can begin to test out whether my fears are really true. 2. I'll stay put if I feel like this again rather than leave the shop, which I did on the last occasion. 3. If I start to overbreathe, I'll close my mouth and take normal-sized breaths at a normal speed through my nose.

Putting the balanced conclusion into practice

Mark completes Column 9 of his Thought Challenge Worksheet, which helps him to consider how he can change what he does to reinforce his balanced conclusion and to undermine his immediate anxious thought by acting against it.

Important point

By far the best evidence for or against an extreme and unhelpful thought is found through looking at the consequences of what happens when you choose to act or not act on it. *Reinforce* balanced conclusions by acting on them. *Undermine* old negative thoughts by acting against them.

Mark puts the three points of his plan into action, and finds that although he feels anxious, this is far less than before. In particular, he did not get anywhere near as dizzy and this helped him to challenge his fears that 'I will faint'.

SUMMARY

This chapter has covered:

- A brief revision of the unhelpful thinking styles and the impact that these have on how you feel and what you do.
- How to 'act like a detective' to carry out a detailed Five Areas Assessment of a specific time when your mood has unhelpfully altered.
- Using a Thought Challenge Worksheet to challenge your own extreme and unhelpful thoughts.
- An example of Anne using her Thought Investigation and Thought Challenge Worksheets to identify and then challenge her unhelpful and extreme thoughts.
- An example of Mark who completes his Thought Investigation Worksheet after a panic attack in a shop. You have also read his Thought Challenge Worksheet that shows him successfully challenging his fear that 'I will faint'.

- A discussion of the importance of putting your balanced conclusion into practice by making changes in what you do.

Putting into practice what you have learned

The important thing is to think about how you can put what you have learned into practice. One way is by praying this prayer and then completing the following tasks over the next week or so.

CLOSING PRAYER

When you can, pray this prayer silently or preferably aloud.

Lord, thank you again for your love for me. I realise that at times I find myself seeing life in negative, extreme and unhelpful ways. Please help me to change this, and I ask that as I begin to use the Thought Investigation and Challenge Worksheets that you will show me how to use them most effectively.

I pray also for all the different people who are reading this book and praying this prayer, that you will help us all to change our own unhelpful thinking. You are the Lord who unblocked ears that couldn't hear, and opened eyes that couldn't see – please help us to see things again in ways that are true, balanced and helpful. Help us to take hold of your promise of love and forgiveness, and to apply this in what we do. Help us to make useful changes in what we do, and to choose to act on your promises. We ask this in Jesus' name.

Amen.

Bible meditation

Remind yourself of what the Bible says about how God sees us, and the completed work of salvation that he has achieved.

- 'For God so loved the world that he gave his one and only Son, that whoever believes in him shall not perish but have eternal life. For God did not send his Son into the world to condemn the world, but to save the world through him' (John 3:16–17).
- 'I tell you the truth, whoever hears my word and believes him who sent me has eternal life and will not be condemned; he has crossed over from death to life' (John 5:24).
- 'In the same way, the Spirit helps us in our weakness. We do not know what we ought to pray for, but the Spirit himself intercedes for us with groans that words cannot express. And he who searches our hearts knows the mind of the Spirit, because the Spirit intercedes for the saints in accordance with God's will' (Romans 8:26–7).
- 'For I am convinced that neither death nor life, neither angels nor demons, neither the present nor the future, nor any powers, neither height nor depth, nor anything else in all creation, will be able to separate us from the love of God that is in Christ Jesus our Lord' (Romans 8:38–9).
- 'Now the Lord is the Spirit, and where the Spirit of the Lord is, there is freedom. And we, who with unveiled faces all reflect the Lord's glory, are being transformed into his likeness with ever increasing glory, which comes from the Lord, who is the Spirit' (2 Corinthians 3:17–18).

Think and pray about each of these passages and consider how you can put what you have learned into practice when it comes to challenging your own extreme and unhelpful thoughts.

Suggested points for action

- Complete your own Thought Investigation and Challenge Worksheets on several occasions each day for the next few weeks to practise these skills. Always choose times when your mood has unhelpfully changed. (Blank copies of both worksheets are printed on pages 276–9).

- Try to complete the worksheets as soon as possible after you notice your mood change so that you have a clear memory of what happened. If you cannot fill them in immediately, try to think yourself back into the situation so that you are as clear as possible in your summary.
- Try to answer all the questions and *stop, think and reflect* as you do this.

You can write out the worksheets or photocopy them for your own use if you wish. Try to carry them around with you in order to help you to identify and challenge any extreme and unhelpful thoughts. With practice you will find that it becomes easier to do this and you will be able to develop more balanced, moderate and helpful thinking.

If you have difficulties with this, don't worry. Just do what you can and discuss any problems you have with someone you trust.

My notes

7

Tackling practical problems and problems of altered behaviour

In Chapter 2, you looked at the different situations, relationship and practical problems that may currently be causing you difficulty:

- Difficult situations: sometimes it can become quite difficult to face certain situations, meet people or go to certain places. This may be because it just seems too hard to do these things because you are feeling so low in mood (an example of *reduced activity*), or because it seems quite scary and you would rather avoid doing things because of your fears (an example of *avoidance*). This latter situation tends to occur in phobias and leads to avoidance of particular people, situations or places such as going into large shops, or into high or crowded places, or into situations where it is difficult to leave, such as being on a bus.
- Relationship problems at home, work, in the church, such as being bullied by a work colleague, ignored by the boss, shouted at by the children.
- Practical difficulties such as housing problems, being in debt, being unemployed, or not being able to pay the bills, etc.

We will cover each of these different areas within this chapter.

One of the main difficulties that people notice when they are feeling depressed or anxious is that they feel overwhelmed by the situations they face. Sometimes it can seem as if you are standing at the foot of a huge mountain of problems, and don't know quite where to start. This chapter will help you to learn a practical Seven-Step Approach to planning how to overcome these problems. The Seven-Step Approach tackles just one problem at a time, and approaches problem solving in an organised and planned way.

THE SEVEN-STEP APPROACH

Step 1: Identify and clearly define the problem you are going to tackle as precisely as possible.
Step 2: Brainstorm as many solutions as possible to overcome the problem.
Step 3: Look at the advantages and disadvantages of each of the possible solutions.
Step 4: Choose one of the solutions.
Step 5: Plan the steps needed to carry it out.
Step 6: Carry out the plan.
Step 7: Review the outcome.

The same Seven-Step Approach can also be used to plan ways of overcoming problems of reduced or avoided activity, or to reduce unhelpful behaviour such as drinking. This chapter is split into three main sections to examine the use of the Seven-Step Approach in each of these areas. You can therefore choose to read those sections that are most helpful for you at the moment. Blank Seven-Step Approach worksheets are provided at the end of the chapter (pages 179–85) so that you can practise this approach yourself.

Before you start

You may have made many previous attempts to change, but unless you have a clear plan and stick to it, change will be difficult. Planning and selecting which areas to try and change first is a crucial part of successfully moving forwards. By choosing which one problem area to focus on initially means that you are actively choosing *not* to focus on other areas.

Setting *targets* will help you to focus on how to make the changes needed to get better. To do this you will need to identify:

- Short-term targets: changes you can make today, tomorrow and next week.
- Medium-term targets: changes to be put in place over the next few weeks.
- Long-term targets: where you want to be in six months or a year.

Think about and answer for yourself the following questions:

Q. What might be the advantage of planning to change just one problem area at first?
Write your answer here:

Q. What are the potential dangers of trying to change *everything* at once?
Write your answer here:

Important principle

If you are facing many different problems, it isn't appropriate or sensible to try to deal with everything at once. In order to tackle them effectively, you need to prioritise and focus on changing just one area to begin with. This means that you may need to decide to put some of your problems on one side at first.

We will come back and think about this some more after we have looked at two examples of the Seven-Step Approach in tackling practical problems and in overcoming difficulties of reduced activity. Even if you aren't currently facing any practical problems, we suggest you read this first section, because it contains important information about how to identify specific targets for change. This will be built upon later in the chapter when you look at ways of overcoming reduced activity/avoidance, and in reducing problem behaviour such as drinking to excess, or other patterns of unhelpful behaviour such as excessive reassurance-seeking.

SECTION 1: PRACTICAL PROBLEM SOLVING?

Let's start by looking in more detail at the Seven-Step Approach and how it can be used to tackle practical problems.

Step 1: Identify and clearly define the problem as precisely as possible

This key step involves defining the problem you are going to tackle and making sure what it is. The important first step is making sure that you have identified a single, focused target problem that is clearly defined. This step is particularly important if you feel overwhelmed by a wide range of different problems. In doing this, it is important to choose a target problem that:

- Will be *useful* for changing how you are.
- Is a *specific* target problem so that you will know when you have done it.
- Is *realistic*: is it practical and achievable?

The Funnel Process: Defining a Specific Problem

One way of thinking about this process of clearly defining the target problem is to think of it as a *funnelling process* – funnelling down from the general problem area to a more specific problem which you tackle first.

Have a look at some examples of this funnelling approach.

Examples: Clearly defining a problem

Completing the funnelling process helps to define a *specific* problem that can then be overcome.

Example 1: Money difficulties

Mark has a *general problem* that 'I don't have enough money'. Although this is a correct statement, it is not a very clear target for change. A more specific target problem might be identified by Mark answering the question, 'Exactly what aspect of not having enough money is causing me a problem at the moment?' By asking this question, Mark is able to define more clearly the problem he wants to tackle first:

Mark's target problem: 'I can't pay my electricity bill this month.'

Example 2: Problems in looking after children

Catherine has two young children at home, and has an unsupportive husband. One of the general problems that she faces is 'I feel stressed by the demands of looking after my children.' Although this is again a correct statement, a more specific target problem might be identified by Catherine answering the question, 'Exactly what aspect of looking after my children is so stressful?' By asking this question, Catherine more clearly defines the problem she wants to tackle first.

Catherine's target problem: 'When the children cry, my husband always expects me to respond to their crying – he never gets up or offers to help.'

If you are stuck when you come to practise this approach a little later, ask yourself, 'Exactly what is it about the general problem that is causing me difficulty?'

As stated already, the problem that is chosen should be one that:

- Will be *useful* for changing how you are.
- Is a *specific* target problem so that you will know when you have done it.
- Is *realistic*: is it practical and achievable?

Step 2: Brainstorm as many solutions as possible to overcome the problem

One difficulty that people often face when they have chosen which problem area to focus on is that they cannot see any ways of dealing with it. It can seem too difficult even to start tackling it. One way around this is to try to step back from the problem and see if any other approaches are possible. This approach is called 'brainstorming'.

In brainstorming:

- The more solutions that are generated, the more likely it is that a good one will emerge.
- Ridiculous ideas should be included as well even if you would never choose them in practice. This can help you to adopt a flexible approach to the problem.

Useful questions to help you to think up possible solutions might include:

- What *ridiculous* solutions can I include as well as more sensible ones?
- What helpful ideas would others (e.g. family, friends at church, the Bible, or colleagues at work) suggest?
- What approaches have I tried in the past in similar circumstances?
- What advice would you give a friend who was trying to tackle the same problem?

Step 3: Look at the advantages and disadvantages of each of the possible solutions

Assess how effective and practical each potential solution is. This involves considering the advantages and disadvantages for each potential solution.

Step 4: Choose one of the solutions

The chosen solution should be an option that will address the problem, and also is realistic and likely to succeed. This decision will be based on your answers to Step 3.

Step 5: Plan the steps needed to carry it out

This is a key stage, and is one that many people have some difficulty completing initially. You need to generate a clear plan that will help you to decide exactly *what* you are going to do and *when* you are going to do it.

It is useful to *write down* the steps needed to carry out the solution and to be specific about what you will do. This will help you to remember what to do and allows you to predict possible blocks and problems that might arise. As you write your plan, ask God to help you plan effectively.

The Questions for Effective Change should always be asked as part of the fifth step of the problem solving approach and can help you to check how practical and achievable your plan is.

The Questions for Effective Change
Is the plan one that:

- Will be *useful* for understanding or changing how I am?
- Is a *specific task* so that I will know when I have done it?
- Is *realistic*: is it practical and achievable?
- Makes clear *what* I am going to do and *when* I am going to do it?
- Is an activity that won't be easily blocked or prevented by practical problems?

If you identify any potential blocks (such as 'What if it rained?' or 'What if they aren't in when I visit?'), how could you overcome this difficulty in a way that still helps you to carry out your plan?

Step 6: Carry out the plan
Once your plan is complete, you should carry it out.

Step 7: Review the outcome
Look at what happened when you carried out your plan. How successful was your plan in tackling your target problem? Did your plan go smoothly, or were there any difficulties along the way? What have you learned from carrying out your plan?

The following simple checklist can aid this review:

Q. Was the selected plan successful?
Q. Did it help solve the target problem?
Q. Were there any disadvantages to using this approach?

Key point: No matter what happens – whether your plan is effective or seems to have failed badly – you can learn from it and take what you have learned into account in your next attempt.

By practising this approach, and constantly reviewing the results, you can begin to learn skills that can be used when approaching *any* practical problems you face. To help you to understand how the approach can be used in practice, the following example shows Mark tackling his own practical problem.

Example

Let's have a look at an example of Mark using this Seven-Step Approach to overcome his problem that 'I don't have enough money'. Mark is a 35-year-old man who is currently feeling depressed. He is self-employed and has been off work and has a reduced income as a result of sick leave.

Step 1: Identify and clearly define the problem you are going to tackle as precisely as possible

You have already seen how Mark used the Funnel Process to decide on his specific target problem.

Mark's target problem: 'I can't pay my electricity bill this month.'

Step 2: Brainstorm as many solutions as possible to overcome the problem

Possible options that Mark identifies are:

- Ignore the problem completely – it may go away.
- Try to borrow the money from someone at church.
- Try to arrange a loan or overdraft from the bank and use this to pay off the bill.
- Speak to the electricity company to ask if they will agree different repayment terms.
- Speak to a counsellor with skills in debt repayments such as the Citizens Advice Bureau.
- Rob a bank!

Step 3: Look at the advantages and disadvantages of each of the possible solutions

Suggestion	Advantages	Disadvantages
Ignore the problem completely – it may go away.	Easier in the short term with no embarrassment.	It will have to be tackled sometime and ignoring it will only make the problem worse.
Try to borrow the money from someone at church.	It might get me some money.	I really don't feel happy about this. I want to try and deal with this myself. It would be embarrassing, and I don't know anyone who has any spare money.
Arrange a loan or overdraft with my bank.	It would certainly sort out the immediate bill.	How would I do this? It would be scary seeing the bank manager. They may also say no. I'm not sure that taking out a loan will help – I'll have to pay that back as well.
Inform the electricity company and ask if they will agree different repayment terms.	It would provide the company with clear information. It's in their best interests for me to keep up the payments. I could spread the payments over a longer time.	It seems quite scary to do this, but a lot less scary than going to the bank.
Speak to a debt counsellor.	I hear they can be very good.	I'd feel embarrassed talking to them. How do you contact them?
Rob a bank.	It might give me the money I need.	It's wrong. I couldn't do that as a Christian. I might go to prison.

Step 4: Choose one of the solutions

Mark decides to inform the electricity company and ask if they will agree different repayment terms. A number of other solutions may have been successful, but Mark decides that this solution is realistic and most likely to work.

Step 5: Plan the steps needed to carry it out

Mark's plan:

> I could phone the electricity company. I have the phone number on my most recent bill. I'm quite nervous so I'm going to plan out what I'm going to say in advance. I'll phone up and tell them I'm having problems repaying my next bill because I am off work sick. I think it's best if I phone them in the afternoon. I'm more likely to get straight through to them then, and I generally feel more confident after lunch.

Mark checks his plan against the questions for effective change, and decides that he has planned effectively. He decides to phone at 2 p.m. that afternoon, and predicts that the line may be engaged when he phones, but that if it is, he won't give up, but instead he will phone back later.

Step 6: Carry out the plan

Mark phones up at 2 p.m. that afternoon as planned. Just before he does this, he feels quite scared. He predicts that the company representative will humiliate him and turn his request down, demanding immediate payment or they will issue a court summons.

Mark decides to try to challenge these fears, prays for strength and phones the company. When he phones the line is engaged. He tries again two minutes later and the phone is answered by an electronic answering service that asks him to make a selection of which service he wants from five options. Mark is surprised by this and is quite taken aback. He becomes flustered and immediately puts the phone down.

His immediate thought is, 'What an idiot! I should be able to do this.' Over the next few minutes, he challenges this thought with the aid of the Thought Challenge Worksheet he had learned to use in Chapter 6. He then decides to learn from what happened and try again (Step 7).

He therefore phones the company again, but plans to have a pen and paper available to write down the different options. He finds that the current option for those with payment difficulties is Option 2. He selects this and is surprised when the line is quickly answered by a friendly voice. She tells him that this is a common problem. Because he has been a customer for a number of years and has a good payment record, there will be no problems sorting things out. She suggests that he moves to a budget scheme with regular monthly payments by direct debit. By doing this Mark can spread the cost throughout the year, rather than paying in two large sums every six months as he currently does. Mark agrees to switch payment schemes, and is happy with how things went. His initial fears of a court summons were completely incorrect. He was able to arrange to pay the bill at a rate that he can afford, and there was no question of a court appearance.

Step 7: Review the outcome

	Mark's review	
Q. Was the selected solution successful?	Yes ✓	No ❑
Q. Did it help pay off the electricity bill (the target problem)?	Yes ✓	No ❑
Q. Were there any disadvantages to using this approach?	Yes ❑	No ✓

Mark's review

In this case, Mark's plan went smoothly the second time he phoned up. Even when a problem arose and he hung up when he phoned on the first occasion, he learned from it and didn't give up. He altered his plan slightly (by getting a pen and paper). Importantly, by phoning back, he not only sorted out his target problem, but he also realised that his extreme and unhelpful fears were quite wrong.

The example used shows how the Seven-Step Approach might be applied to this situation. However, it also works for *any* day-to-day difficulties.

Option If you are facing a practical problem you now have the option of practising this approach if you wish by using the blank Seven-Step Approach worksheets in Section 4 at the end of this chapter.

Another way that the Seven-Step Approach can be used is to overcome problems of altered and unhelpful behaviour, and this is described in the next two sections of the chapter.

SECTION 2: USING THE SEVEN-STEP APPROACH TO OVERCOME REDUCED OR AVOIDED ACTIVITY

Revision

In Chapter 3 you looked at how anxiety and depression may result in a vicious circle of reduced/avoided activity. When you become anxious or depressed, it is normal to find it is difficult to do things.

In depression, this is because of:

- Low energy and tiredness ('I'm too tired').
- Low or anxious mood and little sense of enjoyment or achievement when things are done.
- Negative and worrying thinking and reduced enthusiasm to do things ('I just can't be bothered').

This leads the person to stop doing things that previously gave them a sense of pleasure or achievement. By removing these things the depression worsens.

In anxiety, similar factors may also be present, but an additional factor is that fears may lead the person to avoid facing particular situations, places such as large shops or busy social situations. *Avoidance* is the key here, and the danger is that slowly more and more things are avoided, so that eventually it becomes difficult to do anything.

The result of this is that the person removes many or all of the things from their lives that would normally have provided an important support and would have led to feelings of pleasure and achievement. Life can begin to become emptier and emptier after weeks or months. Soon even everyday things such as getting up and dressed, housework, jobs, and looking after oneself feels like too much to do. In anxiety, the avoidance acts to maintain the problem because the person never comes to realise that their fears aren't true because they never actually face up to doing the things they fear.

A Vicious Circle of Reduced Activity (in Depression) or Avoidance (in Anxiety) May Result

Depression or anxiety with:
- Low/anxious mood.
- Low energy and fatigue.
- Unhelpful thinking styles and reduced motivation *('I just can't be bothered')*.
- Fears *('I can't do that!')*.
- Feeling emotionally distant from God.

Difficulty doing things

Reduced activity: stop going out or meeting people. Stop hobbies and things that were fun. Find reading the Bible and praying difficult.

Avoidance of things that seem scary or too difficult. Avoid specific situations/people/places.

Reduced activity of things that lead to fun/pleasure and a sense of achievement

Reduced activity prevents you from doing potentially helpful things (such as going to mid-week groups/church, meeting with friends, going for walks, etc.). You only do essential jobs.

Avoidance saps your confidence further and restricts places/people/things you are able to do/meet.

Worsen feelings of depression or anxiety

a. Remove pleasure from life
Life becomes emptier and nothing is done that leads to enjoyment. Even essential jobs become too much effort.

b. Life becomes increasingly restricted
Become isolated and lose confidence with others/self. Possibly lose important sources of support. Avoidance leads to an increasingly restricted life ruled by fears.

To help you to work out if this is true for you, ask yourself the question, 'What have I stopped doing since these problems began?'

What you can do to overcome reduced activity

The same Seven-Step Approach can be used to create a plan to overcome problems of reduced/avoided activity. First, let's look at how the Seven-Step Approach can be used to overcome an example of reduced activity.

Step 1: Identify and clearly define the problem as precisely as possible

Anne is 40 years old, lives alone and has been feeling depressed for six months. She has identified that she *generally* needs to 'do more'. She tries to think how she can come up with a more *specific* activity, and realises that she has stopped meeting up with her friends.

> **Anne's target area**: Anne has decided that the specific area of reduced activity that she is going to focus on is that 'I need to start meeting up with my friends again'.

Step 2: Brainstorm as many solutions as possible to overcome the problem

Anne sits and thinks about possible ways she could start to meet up with people again. Read Anne's list below:

- Have street party and invite all the neighbours.
- Ask my sister Mary round again for a cup of tea.
- Phone my friend Sarah.

Step 3: Look at the advantages and disadvantages of each of the possible solutions

Suggestion	Advantages	Disadvantages
1. Have a street party and invite all the neighbours.	I'd meet lots of people.	The idea is too scary. It would be too hard getting ready for it. I couldn't cope with it at the moment.
2. Ask my sister Mary round again.	I always used to enjoy her visits and I do miss her company.	That could be nice as long as she didn't stay too long. I do worry that she'll ask me too many questions about how I am though.
3. Phone my friend Sarah.	We used to get on well and enjoyed meeting each other.	I haven't spoken to her for ages and it would be difficult explaining why I have phoned now.

Step 4: Choose one of the solutions
Anne decides on Option 2 – to ask her sister Mary round. Option 3 (to phone her friend Sarah) might also have been possible, but on balance Anne prefers Option 2 as this is more likely to be a realistic, practical and achievable target.

Step 5: Plan the steps needed to carry it out
Anne uses the Questions for Effective Change to help her plan her task.

The Questions for Effective Change

1. Will it be useful for understanding or changing how I am?
'Even though I worry what Mary will think of me, it will be useful for me to face up to my worries and ask her to come over. I think that is an important thing for me to change and it will get me socialising again with someone I like.'

2. Is it a specific task so that I will know when I have done it?
'I'm clear what I am going to do – I'll invite her round one afternoon in the next week.'

3. Is it realistic: is it practical and achievable?
'Is it realistic – yes, I could do that, she's been round a lot before and we get on well. I feel a little bit nervous about it, but I think I am probably just mind-reading again' (see Chapter 2).

4. Does it make clear what I am going to do and when I am going to do it?
'I could phone Mary up now and arrange it. I'll invite her for a specific afternoon – this Tuesday at 2.00 p.m. – but just for an hour. I'd feel too tired if it was for any longer.'

5. Is it an activity that won't be easily blocked or prevented by practical problems?
'Now then, what might block it? Maybe Mary won't be in when I phone. If so, I'll phone again later. Perhaps she'll be busy on Tuesday, after all, she has such a busy life. If so, I'll ask her to come another day. If she isn't able to come then, I'm not going to take it personally. Instead I'll ask her again for later this week. The only other thing that I can predict could prevent me doing this is if I lose my nerve and think about cancelling her on the day, but I think it will be all right. I'm usually feeling at my best in the afternoon. As long as I tell her that it's just for an hour to begin with I think that will be fine. I'm going to invite her right now.'

Anne's goals are clear, specific and realistic. She knows what she is going to do and when she is going to do it. She has predicted potential difficulties that might get in the way. This seems like a well-thought-through plan.

Step 6: Carry out the plan

Anne phones Mary who says she is delighted to hear from Anne. She says she has been worried about how Anne is and wants to visit. They arrange to meet on Tuesday afternoon.

Step 7: Review the outcome

Anne challenges her negative predictions that it will be really embarrassing meeting again, and that her sister will ask too many questions about how she feels. In fact, none of her fears come true and they both get on really well. Anne feels really supported by what Mary says, and they arrange to meet again for slightly longer next week. Overall, Anne realises that she *has* gained some pleasure from meeting Mary, and a definite sense of achievement.

	Anne's review	
Q. Was the selected approach successful?	Yes ✓	No ❑
Q. Did it help Anne to start meeting up with people again (the target problem)?	Yes ✓	No ❑
Q. Were there any disadvantages to using this approach?	Yes ❑	No ✓

In this case Anne's plan went smoothly. Even if there had been a problem, she could have learned from what had happened and used this to improve her next plan.

Building on what you have learned – putting together a longer-term plan

You may remember that at the start of this chapter we mentioned that sometimes during times of anxiety or depression it can seem as if you are standing at the foot of a huge mountain of problems, and don't know quite where to start in order to overcome them. However, a large mountain can be climbed if you tackle it one step at a time. The Seven-Step Approach provides you with a clear structure to plan each step of the way.

The next key stage is to build each step upon the previous one so that you have a clear plan and are able to move things forward. To do this, you need to think about your short-, medium- and longer-term targets/goals.

- Short-term targets: changes you can make today, tomorrow and the next week.
- Medium-term targets: changes to be put in place over the next few weeks.
- Long-term targets: where you want to be in six months or a year.

The key is to build one step upon another, so that each time you plan out and complete the Seven-Step Approach you can then consider the next step you should be taking. Without this sort of longer-term strategy you may find that although you take some steps, these are all in different directions and you lose your focus and motivation as a result.

Example: Creating a longer-term strategy to overcome problems of avoiding shopping

Mark is experiencing panic attacks whenever he goes to a supermarket. He has started to avoid going to supermarkets and larger shops as a result. Mark's specific target is 'to be able to go shopping in the supermarket by myself'.

Mark plans out the different steps that he needs to complete over the next few weeks using the step-by-step approach.

Initial Fear level		Time scale
0%	Standing outside the local shop.	Week 1
	↓	
10%	Going into the local shop for a paper.	Week 2
	↓	
40%	Queuing in the post office.	Week 3
	↓	
50%	Going into local shops while they are busy.	Week 4
	↓	
70%	Going into the supermarket foyer area and staying there.	Week 5
	↓	
100%	Going shopping in the supermarket by myself.	Week 6

You can see that his medium-term plan is in fact made up of six separate steps – and each step can be planned out in detail using the Seven-Step Approach. Each step builds on the previous one to help him to move forwards. Over a number of weeks this can add up to a very significant total change in what he is able to do.

In completing each step he also needs to be careful that he doesn't subtly avoid facing up to his fear when he is in the shop – for example, by rushing round the shop as quickly as possible, or going shopping only when accompanied by a friend so that he feels safer. Instead, he should walk round the shop deliberately slowly, having a good look around, allowing himself to experience the anxiety, but not hurrying away. By doing this he will find that his anxiety level begins slowly to fall, and each time he repeats this, the anxiety will be less intense, and last for a shorter time. The plan helps Mark to face up to his fear in a graded and paced way, so that he never feels so anxious that he wants to give up. By repeating each new stage several times each week, Mark can build up his confidence before moving on to the next step as planned the following week. If he finds that a particular stage is too difficult, he can always take a step back, and re-plan the next task so that it is aiming to do something that is more attainable for him at that time. By succeeding in these planned steady steps, real progress can be achieved.

At the same time Mark needs to plan to reduce any unhelpful reassurance-seeking. For example, Mark feels safer if he goes shopping with his sister. He could build this into his plan by, for example, planning first of all to go to the local shop with his sister, and do this repeatedly until he feels less anxious, and then keep doing this while his sister stands further and further away from the shop, until finally he can do this task without her being there at all. Actions like these are sometimes called 'safety behaviours' – because they lead you to feel safer, at least in the short term. In the longer term, however, they actually add to your problems by undermining your confidence. You will find out more about safety behaviours shortly.

This same approach where each step builds upon previous ones can be successfully used to:

- Re-introduce more activities that lead to a sense of pleasure and achievement.
- Overcome avoidance that has occurred as a result of anxieties or phobias such as a fear of spiders, heights, going on buses or talking to others.
- Help plan a reduction in a single unhelpful behaviour such as drinking, excessive reassurance-seeking or trying to spend your way out of depression. This is explained in the next section.

SECTION 3: OVERCOMING UNHELPFUL BEHAVIOURS

Revision

In Chapter 3, you found that sometimes people with anxiety or depression may try to block how they feel by using unhelpful behaviour such as:

- Safety behaviours such as seeking constant reassurance from others or becoming very dependent on them to do things to help (such as the shopping).
- Misusing alcohol or drugs to block how they feel.
- Becoming very irritable and pushing others away.
- Self-harming as a way of blocking unpleasant emotions.
- Trying to spend their way out of how they feel – sometimes called 'retail therapy'.

These changes may add to their problems because although they may feel slightly better in the short term, in the longer term such actions act to worsen the problems. A vicious circle of unhelpful behaviour may arise as a result.

A useful question in order to identify unhelpful behaviours is to ask yourself, 'What am I *doing differently* to cope with how I feel?'

The same Seven-Step Approach can also be used to overcome unhelpful behaviours. By working through the seven steps, you can learn an approach that enables you to reduce any problem behaviours.

Example: Creating a longer-term strategy to overcome problems of drinking too much

John has realised he has a *general* problem that he is drinking too much. John's specific target is that he wants to reduce his drinking to only two glasses of wine a week over the next two months. He needs to write a clear step-by-step plan that is likely to be successful. He sees his doctor to discuss this, and together they agree the following strategy.

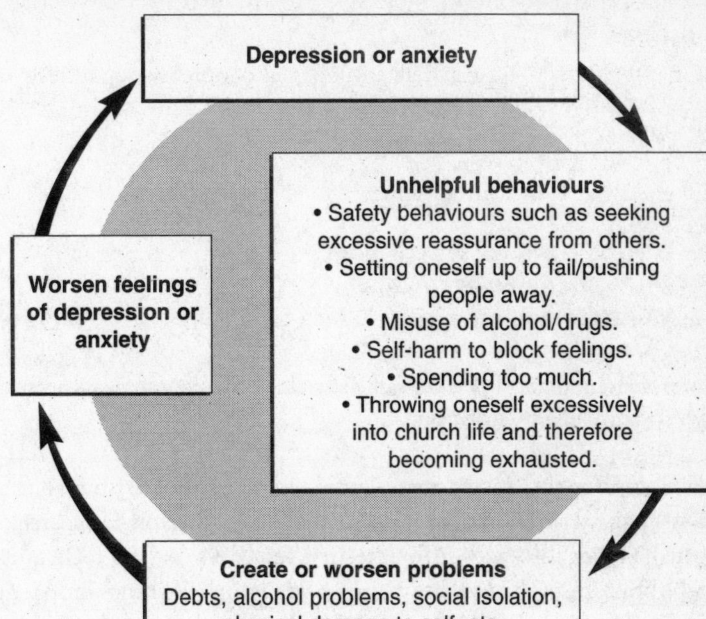

JOHN'S STRATEGY

Problem behaviour: drinking too much	**Units/week***	**Time**
Drinking 3 bottles of wine at home by myself four times a week.	72 units	Week 1
↓		
Drinking 2 bottles of wine at home four times a week.	48 units	Week 2
↓		
Drinking 2 bottles of wine at home three times a week.	36 units	Week 3
↓		
Drinking 1.5 bottles of wine at home three times a week.	27 units	Week 4

↓		
Drinking 1 bottle of wine at home three times a week.	18 units	Week 5
↓		
Drinking 4 glasses of wine at home three times a week.	12 units	Week 6
↓		
Drinking 2 glasses of wine at home twice a week.	4 units	Week 7
↓		
Target behaviour: drinking only 1 glass of wine twice a week	2 units	Week 8

*Note: one unit of alcohol is the same as a glass of wine, a single short such as whisky, or half a pint of beer.

John then uses the Seven-Step Approach to plan each step so that he has a clear written plan of what he will do each week. He manages to put his plan into action for the first few days and he feels quite good about himself and how things are going. Things don't go according to plan, though, when John goes to a work party. He has two cans to drink, and then thinks, 'What the heck, let your hair down.' He ends up drinking ten pints of beer in a binge and has to take a taxi home. The next day he wakes up feeling worse and thinks about giving up the planned reduction in drinking completely. After a few hours, he begins to think about what he had learned before from his doctor about having to stick to a clear plan if he is going to succeed. He also remembers his doctor telling him that it is likely there will be occasional hiccups, but that it can still work out for the good – he can learn from what happens and plan to avoid making the same mistake again. Just because a setback occurs doesn't mean that everything is over. John therefore tries again and restarts his plan. He finds that he is able to reach his target over the next few weeks.

Key point: John's medium-term plan is in fact made up of a number of separate steps – in this case eight steps – and each step can be planned out in detail using the Seven-Step Approach. Each one builds on the previous ones to help him to move forwards. Over a number of weeks this can add up to a very significant total change in what he is able to achieve.

You now have the opportunity to try this approach yourself.

SECTION 4: PUTTING INTO PRACTICE WHAT YOU HAVE LEARNED – CREATING YOUR OWN SEVEN-STEP APPROACH

The final section of this chapter will allow you to try putting what you have learned into practice. To begin with, think about your short-, medium- and longer-term targets. The Seven-Step Approach can help you to plan to put the first step of your longer-term strategy into action.

Step 1: Identify and clearly define the problem you are going to tackle as precisely as possible

This first key step involves defining the problem area that you are going to tackle and making sure that it is clear and focused. This step is particularly important if you have a number of possible targets that you could tackle.

Think about which area you want to tackle first. This may be to:

- Re-introduce some activities that lead to a sense of pleasure and achievement.
- Overcome an area of avoidance that has been caused by problems of anxiety or a phobia such as a fear of spiders, heights, going on buses or talking to others, etc.
- Help plan a reduction in a single unhelpful behaviour such as spending too much to cheer you up, excessive reassurance-seeking or drinking too much.

You have to choose which area you want to tackle first – and by implication which other areas you will not focus on at present. Choosing the right target and making sure that is an area that is possible to change is important – there must be a realistic chance of success.

The crucial thing in clearly defining which area to focus upon is to be *specific*. Use the Funnel Process to come up with a more specific target activity.

Example: Using the Funnel Process to define a more specific problem	
'General' problem	**'Specific' problem** The problem should be one that: 1. Will be *useful* for changing how you are. 2. Is a *specific* target problem so that you will know when you have done it. 3. Is *realistic*: is it practical and achievable?
Example: I have difficulties with colleagues at work.	Q. *Exactly what about your job is causing you a problem?* e.g. I am the person who always ends up washing all the coffee mugs.
Example: I'm having problems with my neighbour.	Q. *Exactly what does your neighbour do that causes you a problem?* e.g. His son plays his music loud every night until 1 a.m.

Now apply this same principle to help you to identify your own *general* and more *specific* targets.

Write your own general and specific target below:

My 'general' problem area	**My 'specific' problem area**
✎	(Write in **one** target only) ✎

When you have completed this Funnel Process you need to check that the chosen activity is one that:

1. Will be useful for changing how you are.
2. Is a specific target problem so that you will know when you have done it.
3. Is realistic: is it practical and achievable?

You should *avoid*

- Choosing something that is too ambitious a target to start with.
- Trying to start to alter too many things all at once.
- Being very negative and thinking 'nothing can be done'.

If you think that you have been too ambitious, rewrite the specific area you have identified above in less ambitious terms.

Step 2: Brainstorm as many solutions as possible to overcome the problem

Think up as many possible solutions as you can. Include ridiculous solutions as well as more sensible ones. This can help you to adopt a flexible approach to the problem. Useful questions to help you to think up possible solutions might include:

- What ridiculous solutions can I include as well as more sensible ones?
- What helpful ideas would others (e.g. family, friends at church, the Bible or colleagues at work) suggest?
- What approaches have I tried in the past in similar circumstances?
- What advice would I give a friend who was trying to tackle the same problem?

Try to create as many ideas as you can. If this proves difficult, try to think of some bizarre ideas first to help get your ideas flowing.

Brainstorming my problem

Possible options (including ridiculous ideas at first) are:

Step 3: Look at the advantages and disadvantages of each of the possible solutions

Assess how effective and practical each potential solution is. This involves considering the advantages and disadvantages for each solution.

Suggestion	Advantages	Disadvantages

Suggestion	Advantages	Disadvantages

Step 4: Choose one of the solutions

The chosen solution should be an option that is realistic and likely to be successful. This decision will be based on your answers to Step 3.

The solution should be an option that fulfils the following two criteria:

1. Is it helpful? Yes ❑ No ❑
2. Is it achievable? Yes ❑ No ❑

Step 5: Plan the steps needed to carry it out

Write down the practical steps needed to carry out your plan. Try to be very specific in your plan so that you know what you are going to do, and when you are going to do it.

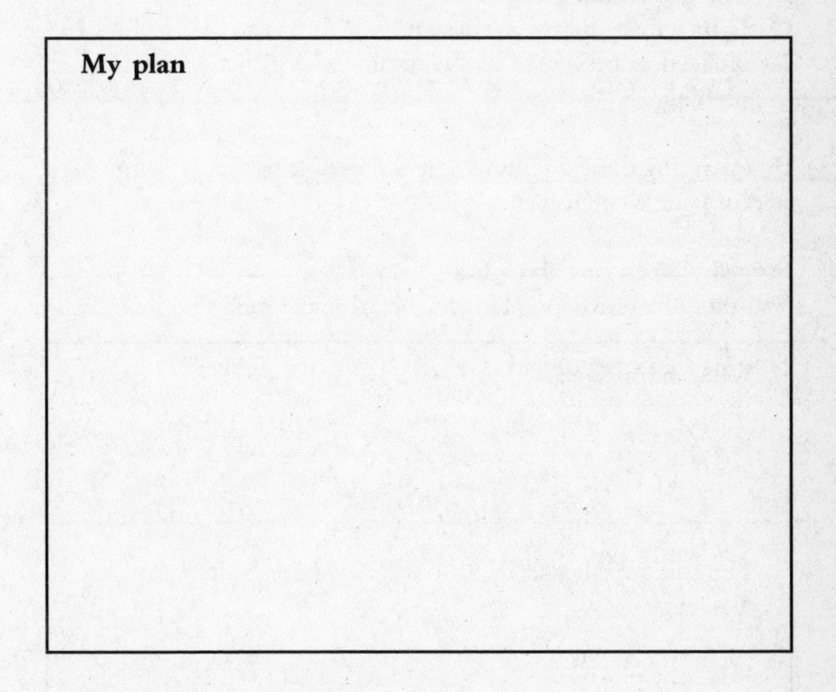

Be as precise as possible in your plan. Try to predict possible problems and work out how to avoid or deal with them.

Next, apply the Questions for Effective Change to your plan to check how practical and achievable it is:

Is my planned task one that:

Q. Will be useful for understanding or changing how I am?	Yes ❑	No ❑
Q. Is a specific task so that I will know when I have done it?	Yes ❑	No ❑
Q. Is realistic: is it practical and achievable?	Yes ❑	No ❑
Q. Makes clear what I am going to do and when I am going to do it?	Yes ❑	No ❑
Q. Is an activity that won't be easily blocked or prevented by practical problems?	Yes ❑	No ❑

By answering these questions you will be able to clearly define each step of your written plan.

Step 6: Carry out the plan

You should aim to complete your plan at the time you intended.

What happened

Step 7: Review the outcome

Q. Was the selected solution successful? Yes ❑ No ❑

Q. Did it help deal with the target problem? Yes ❑ No ❑

Q. Were there any disadvantages to using this approach? Yes ❑ No ❑

Q. What have I learned from doing this?

Task: Write down any helpful lessons or information you have learned from what happened. If things didn't go quite as you hoped, try to learn from this. How could you make things different during your next attempt to tackle the problem?

My review

Repeated practice of the Seven-Step Approach is important and you will find that you gain skills in doing this.

Summary

The Seven-Step Approach is an effective technique to help in solving practical problems.

It can be used to:

- Re-introduce more activities that lead to a sense of pleasure and achievement.
- Overcome avoidance that has occurred as a result of anxieties or phobias such as a fear of spiders, heights, going on buses or talking to others, etc.
- Help plan a reduction in an unhelpful behaviour such as drinking, excessive reassurance-seeking or trying to spend your way out of depression.

Try to learn from any mistakes and keep practising so that using this approach becomes second nature whenever you face a problem. If you think that your first attempt has been unsuccessful don't give up; review what you have done and learn from it; perhaps share your experience with someone you trust.

Putting what you have learned into practice

Choose one or two problem areas and use the Seven-Step Approach yourself over the next few weeks.

As you finish reading this chapter, you may want to reflect on what you have learnt. Think of the Seven-Step Approach, the Funnel Process and how you are going to put your plan into action. Spend a few minutes in silence before God and think about the problems you are facing; perhaps make a list and 'offer' them to God. Consider each one in the light of how big and powerful God is and in the light of Jesus' words that small amounts of faith can remove entire mountains.

As you do this, the following prayer may be helpful.

Closing prayer

When you can, pray this prayer silently or preferably aloud.

Father,
I bring before you all my problems. I thank you that however numerous and daunting my difficulties look to me right now, none of them is too big in your eyes. Thank you that even though sometimes I find it hard to trust you in my difficulties, you will never let go of me.

I want to bring to you the problems that I am facing. If there are any that have come about because I have disobeyed you I want to say I am sorry and to receive your forgiveness.

I thank you for all I have read in this chapter. I thank you that this approach can help me to focus on my difficulties and help me to solve them.

Help me to focus on the first area to target. Give me the strength to use the Seven-Step Approach. Help me to define the problem clearly, to brainstorm and come up with really helpful solutions. Give me wisdom to chose one solution and help me as I work on the plan to carry this out. If there are difficulties, help me to overcome them. If I think I have failed, reassure me and help me to try again.

Please help all the other people who are reading this chapter and who are trying to work through the Seven-Step Approach to overcoming their problems. Thank you that you will be with them as they do this, and that it will be easier as a result. Help them to find workable steps to take to overcome these things, and please give them the joy of seeing many difficulties resolved. Reassure them of your presence, help and strength.

Help us not to give up if things don't go well at first, but to persevere, and learn from our mistakes.

I pray that there will be many victories because of what I and others have learned.

I thank you that through you all things are possible.

Thank you, Lord. Amen.

My notes

8

How to get the most from your church when you are feeling anxious or depressed

The aim of this chapter is to help you plan ways of getting the most helpful support that is possible from your own church and Christian friends. The resources that exist in most churches to support and help those who are depressed and anxious are potentially enormous. There are dozens, maybe hundreds, of people who believe in following Jesus' command to love one another as he has loved us. There are full-time or part-time ministers trained in pastoral care; there may be house group leaders, lay leaders, elders, deacons, ministry teams and any number of people who may be able to offer help and support.

For someone experiencing depression or anxiety there should be great comfort in knowing that all these resources are potentially available, and the local church ought to be a source of hope, encouragement and support. At its best the church is all of this and more, a tremendous asset to people experiencing depression or anxiety; assisting in recovery and restoration for as long as it takes to regain good mental health. However, in order to access this support, we need to feel free to discuss how we feel with others. An important factor that may prevent this discussion is our own fear and concern about the stigma surrounding mental health issues, which can sometimes make us choose to avoid discussing our difficulties with others.

The stigma of mental health problems

Even in the twenty-first century, there is still a surprising amount of stigma surrounding mental illness. People sometimes have preconceived and inaccurate ideas about mental illness. Strangely, if a Christian develops a physical illness they do not normally think that this is due to a lack of faith, yet such comments are not uncommon about mental health difficulties. This is not surprising since churches consist of other human beings with flaws, prejudices, misunderstanding and even ignorance about things like anxiety and depression, and this can cause considerable difficulties.

Sadly, in relation to mental health we frequently encounter an alarming lack of understanding among those delivering pastoral care and ministry. Coupled with this there are still some fundamental myths about mental health problems that are held by a number of Christians – including some in leadership – that are likely to result in those experiencing anxiety and depression feeling misunderstood, rejected and inadequate. The tragedy of this situation is that the intentions of those who respond unhelpfully are almost always good; it is simply a lack of understanding of mental health issues that creates an environment that is unhealthy or even damaging for those experiencing depression or anxiety. Chapter 10 is particularly written for church leaders and those who are likely to minister to people experiencing poor mental health, but you may also find it useful to read yourself.

What are the main problems that we can experience in our relationship with others in our church?

Potential problems in our relationships with others in our church

We have seen in earlier chapters that our thinking patterns can become quite extreme and unhelpful when we are experiencing depression or anxiety. They alter our view of ourselves, other people and God. In particular we can focus a great deal on aspects of ourselves that we see in a negative light and ignore completely the more positive things. This is a common experience for most people when feeling depressed or anxious whether or not they have a personal faith, but for the Christian there are one or two areas that can cause particular problems; these are feelings of *false guilt* and *low self-esteem*.

The problem of false guilt

Among the most fundamental and basic beliefs of most Christians are these:

- Everyone is guilty before God of sin: 'All have sinned and fallen short of the glory of God' (Romans 3:23, NRSV).
- Jesus died for our sin to set us free from condemnation and give us salvation: 'For while we were still weak, at the right time Christ died for the ungodly . . . But God proves his love for us in that while we still were sinners Christ died for us' (Romans 5:6, 8, NRSV).

The Christian faith accepts that guilt is a normal response when we have broken God's laws. In the normal course of events guilt is a helpful part of the cycle of sin, repentance, forgiveness and restoration. However, if we develop mental health problems such as anxiety or depression, this normal helpful cycle can become disrupted. Psychologists and psychiatrists have found that during periods of anxiety and depression, people may unhelpfully and incorrectly feel guilty about things that are either not their fault, or about which they have already been forgiven by God. As a result, feelings of guilt cause them to feel that they are utter failures.

Howard Gordon is a Baptist minister who has worked for many years as a hospital chaplain with people experiencing depression, and has written particularly about the issue of guilt. He relates a typical conversation with someone experiencing depression like this:

Patient	I feel so guilty.
Chaplain	God is willing to forgive everybody's wrongdoing.
Patient	Yes, I know that.
Chaplain	Have you asked God to forgive you?
Patient	Yes, I have.
Chaplain	Do you believe that he has forgiven you?
Patient	Yes, I do.
Chaplain	Then what is the problem?
Patient	I don't *feel* forgiven. [italics added]*

Howard Gordon goes on to discuss different types of guilt feelings, and particularly the difference between true and appropriate guilt – where moral and legal rules have been broken – and false guilt, where there is no real personal responsibility for the things we feel guilty about.

It is this 'false guilt' that is so often present when we feel anxious or depressed, and in spite of our belief that God forgives our wrongdoing we just don't *feel* as if it has happened.

Exercise

Are there particular things that you are feeling guilty about at the moment?

Yes ❑ No ❑

*Taken from an unpublished PhD thesis, 'Christian Identity and the Alleviation of Guilt Feelings in Depressive Illness', Cranfield University School of Management, November 1996, p. 19. Reproduced with the permission of H. Gordon.

If there are, write them down here:

Now go back over what you have written and ask yourself and God if you are *really* responsible for wrongdoing in these areas. Is this an example of false guilt caused by anxiety or depression – where you judge yourself as guilty just because you *feel* guilty – even though these feelings are directly caused by the mental health problem itself?

Consider asking a Christian friend whom you trust to help you with this exercise. It may help to hear someone else state with confidence that some of the things you currently feel very guilty about are in fact based purely on feeling, rather than being based on something you should feel guilty about.

Key point: Where there are things that we can clearly see have been wrong with our lives it is right to confess those things to God and receive forgiveness. Sometimes it can help if we are able to share these things with a Christian friend we trust with confidential information. It may help to hear someone else state with confidence that God has removed our sin from us. This idea of believing that things are true simply because they *feel* like they are true is sometimes called 'emotional reasoning'. Emotions are very important aspects of all our lives, but it is also important to be aware that during times of depression and anxiety our thinking and emotions may become biased and distorted. You may then feel guilty for things that you are not really responsible for. It is important to recognise that this is a symptom of your condition, and if so that this feeling of false guilt will disappear as you recover from your depressed or anxious mood.

Sometimes your church can unwittingly aggravate, or even cause, feelings of false guilt. For example in the preaching of sermons that emphasise the fundamental truths of the gospel we mentioned earlier, these truths can be distorted by our low mood so that we focus upon aspects such as condemnation; and the forgiveness and love of God are overlooked – an example of the so-called 'negative mental filter' you read about in Chapter 2 of this book. The Bible speaks about God's unconditional forgiveness as well as his judgment, yet we may filter out the positive and fail to recognise this when we feel depressed or anxious. This may also cause us to overlook another very important truth about our relationship with God – the fact that we have been justified by what he has done.

The importance of justification

The biblical idea of justification means 'to treat as' or 'to make righteous'. The New Testament word for 'justification' is formed from the same word as that for 'righteousness'. The point is that God doesn't just forgive our sin; he also regards us as being sinless and righteous. This isn't because he has a defective memory, but because of the great love he has for us.

We looked earlier at Romans 3:23 where Paul speaks of everyone having sinned and fallen short of God's glory. Lots of people know this verse, but fewer know that verse 24 says this: 'They are now justified by his grace as a gift, through the redemption that is in

Christ Jesus' (NRSV). Of course reading this verse may not suddenly make you feel 'forgiven', but it may help to reassure you that your feelings of unforgiveness are not from God, and are more than likely a symptom of your current emotional state – another example of emotional reasoning.

However you feel, and however much you think you are failing the expectations of those you share fellowship with, you are not a failure in God's eyes simply because you are experiencing anxiety or depression. Try to remember this, because otherwise you will end up carrying a far heavier load than you would otherwise, and this is likely to hinder rather than help your recovery.

Understanding low self-esteem

Closely related to the difficulties we may experience in feeling forgiven is that of how we regard our value in God's eyes. Part of anxiety and depression is to bring to the surface deeply rooted self-doubts and self-criticism. Thoughts where we judge ourselves as complete failures or where we see ourselves as totally worthless, bad and damaged may begin to occur more and more frequently during anxiety and depression, and become harder to challenge and dismiss from mind. We can sometimes begin to look for comments and experiences that confirm these negative judgments about ourselves. This negative mental filter can alter our view of how we think others see us, and also how we assume God sees us.

How low self-worth affects our view of how others see us

During times of depression and anxiety we often end up feeling useless, awkward or even a fraud as a Christian. You may also be concerned about what other people in church think of you, for example that they will talk about you in negative terms, or that you will be treated with too much sympathy. These fears will vary a great deal from person to person; however, common concerns result from mind-reading and self-doubt. In reality very few in your fellowship will think this way about people with poor mental health, and we are simply misreading the way they think about us. Try to recognise that the great majority of people in your church will accept you as you are and only want the best for you. The chance look or the casual remark are most unlikely to carry the negative significance you may attach to them when feeling low or anxious.

You may recognise this kind of doubt in yourself when in church with people you have previously felt very comfortable with. However, generally speaking the impression that folk huddled together in a group are talking about you is just that – an impression – fed by some of the negative thoughts you are having about yourself. It is far more likely that they are talking about the condition of the church drains or the latest football results.

How low self-worth affects our view of how God sees us

A similar difficulty can be that we think that even God accepts us only reluctantly and with little enthusiasm or love. In reality, when God receives us it is as children and heirs rather than as orphans and beggars. This is one of the messages of the parable of the prodigal son in Luke 15:11–31. The wayward son had wasted away his share of his father's inheritance, and decided to return home with a carefully prepared speech: 'Father, I have sinned against heaven and before you; I am no longer worthy to be called your son; treat me like one of your hired hands' (NRSV). His father, however, scanning the horizon for his lost son, saw him coming in the distance, ran to him, put his arms around him and kissed him. Cutting short the carefully prepared speech the father instructed the servants:

> Quickly, bring out a robe – the best one – and put it on him; put a ring on his finger and sandals on his feet. And get the fatted calf and kill it, and let us eat and celebrate; for this son of mine was dead and is alive again; he was lost and is found!

These three items of clothing are significant; the finest robe speaks about the status of sonship, the ring is an emblem of authority, and the shoes imply a free man rather than a slave.

> **Key point:** Our status in God's eyes is that of children and heirs of God. We have the authority of God to live as his children and to have freedom from condemnation and the consequences of our sinful nature. If you judge yourself as useless, worthless, and a burden rather than an asset to God, it is really important to recognise that these feelings are just that – feelings that are a symptom of how you see yourself rather than God's view.
>
> Difficulties of ruminating over feelings of guilt and self-worth mostly reduce or disappear completely as you recover from depression and anxiety. If you are feeling like this it may help to keep some of the Bible verses that we have mentioned near you so that you can reread them regularly and be reassured that however guilty and worthless you are feeling, that is not how God sees you.

Keeping going to church

One of the difficult things for a Christian experiencing depression or anxiety is that even the previously simple and straightforward components of their Christian life can suddenly seem hard.

Often people with depression find it difficult to keep going to church. Disturbed patterns of sleep and low energy during the daytime are frequent symptoms of depression and may leave you feeling that you simply lack the energy or motivation to go anywhere that is not absolutely vital, and certainly not to church. You may possibly feel intimidated simply by being in an enclosed space with a lot of other people. You may feel under pressure to conform to a particular image such as wearing a smile, hugging lots of people and so on. Depending on the type of church you attend you may find the environment difficult. A church with a lot of young families where children are allowed some liberty to run around and make noise may be ideal for many people, but a lot of bodies and substantial amounts of noise and movement can leave you feeling rather insecure and vulnerable if you are experiencing poor mental health. An older, dark building can be a quite depressing place to go, even if others think that it is absolutely beautiful and reflects something of the glory of God.

At times you will almost certainly feel like avoiding church, not because of a lack of belief but because of the demands this makes on you to interact with people while there. It may be that you find it difficult to face people and have problems of low confidence or anxiety. On one level it is important to recognise that all these experiences are a normal part of suffering from anxiety or depression, but having said that, unless your feelings of depression and anxiety are made worse by attending church it is almost always better to go. A difficulty in giving up church attendance is that it simply becomes harder the next time around, until after several weeks it may become really difficult to walk through the door. Suddenly 'church attendance' has become an issue, and consequently just one more thing to worry about.

What you can do

Reduce your church commitments to an appropriate level given how unwell you feel

- Try to persevere in going to church, though be realistic about what you expect of yourself when feeling anxious or depressed.
- If you normally go to church twice on Sundays, and this now seems difficult, go to only one of the services for a time. If you find it difficult to make conversation, then plan to arrive just as the service is starting, and consider leaving as soon as it ends. If you do this, it may be useful to let your church leadership know why you are doing this in order to avoid misunderstanding.

Go to a quieter service if this is helpful

Many churches have more than one service on a Sunday, and sometimes during the week too, and it may be worthwhile considering going to something other than the 'main' service – usually mid-morning on Sundays. Sunday evening services, for example, are often quieter, more reflective and attended by fewer people. Children are generally absent from these services too. If your church has a service like this you may find it easier to attend than the 'main' service.

Choose which mid-week group to go to

What is true about church in general can also be said about small groups, such as Bible study or house groups. These can be a tremendous support and a great source of practical, emotional and spiritual help, but there will undoubtedly be times when you will lack the energy to go. If you are a part of such a group it is probably best to tell the leader about what is happening so that she or he can encourage and pray for you, and be understanding when you really feel under the weather.

Making these changes will help ensure that your church involvement helps rather than hinders how you feel.

ESTABLISHING HELPFUL AND SUPPORTIVE RELATIONSHIPS WITHIN YOUR CHURCH

As a Christian you are probably a member of a local church. Churches come in all sizes, shapes and styles, and amid this bewildering variety of possibilities it is not easy to make general rules that will apply in each case. You may attend a new church or one that has been in existence for more than a thousand years, one that has a traditional clergyman complete with dog collar and cassock or one where the leaders are more informally addressed by their first names. Worship may be quiet and reflective, liturgical, or free and lively.

All these differences are as much about style and preference as anything else, and hopefully the fellowship to which you belong will be one in which you feel able to be yourself, that suits your personality and is able to support and care for those who belong to it. Unless you live in a small village with no independent means of transport it is extremely unlikely that you will only have one fellowship to choose from. Hopefully you belong to your church because it is both the place where you sense God wants you to serve him and because it offers the kind of support and pastoral care you need.

Churches are all about relationships. A major reason for the creation of the Church was so that God's people could worship him, learn about him and relate to him together rather than as isolated individuals. Churches that are most effective at caring for their members are generally those that have healthy and supportive relationships involving qualities such as honesty, availability, vulnerability and accountability. To be offered help, however, you need to let others know how you feel.

Tell your church leaders

If you have been diagnosed as suffering from depression or anxiety one of the first things to do is to let your church leadership know, but this is often one of the most difficult things to face. You may experience feelings of failure, embarrassment or guilt, or fear that they will simply not understand how you feel.

Perhaps you are reluctant to let your church leaders know about how you feel because you are afraid what they will think of you as a result.

Common fears:

- I will be condemned for my lack of faith and commitment.
- Perhaps they will simply not understand how I feel.
- My difficulties will become known by the entire church who will then discuss all my personal problems.
- Maybe I will be forced to undergo some form of counselling or ministry that frightens me.

While it is true, sadly, that these reactions occasionally occur, the vast majority of clergy and lay leaders are in the positions they occupy because they have both a desire to help people in need and because God has entrusted a 'flock' to them. The great majority will be understanding, sympathetic and supportive, and do all they can to help in the process of restoring you to good mental health. Your diagnosis should not become the subject of church gossip and the ministry you receive will be gentle and loving. This cannot happen, however, if you do not tell your church leadership about your condition.

Q. Have you told any fellow Christians or your church leaders that you are feeling anxious or depressed?

If not, try to work out why. What are your thoughts and fears about what might happen if you told them?

Q. How could telling a fellow Christian/church leader be helpful for you and for them?

Q. Who in my church fellowship could I trust with this information?

If possible, make a definite plan to speak to them about it – perhaps when you reach the end of this chapter.

Avoid or reduce your exposure to 'unhelpful' relationships

Having people around who can share with you and support you until you recover is a great advantage in dealing with anxiety and depression. The right kind of friendship and support, particularly if it comes from another Christian, can helpfully assist the process of recovery a great deal. On the other hand, sometimes the 'support' that is offered – no matter how well-intentioned – is quite unhelpful. Unhelpful relationships are ones that worsen how you feel.

It is important that you think carefully about which people you choose to spend time with when you are feeling unwell, the amount of time you spend with them, and the type of input you receive from them. This is especially important in the area of friendships, and may mean choosing to relate mostly to those who will have a helpful influence on you and choosing to keep at arm's length for a time those whose input is more unhelpful and worsens how you feel.

Two particular unhelpful relationships to avoid are:

Gathering around you people who are currently depressed or anxious themselves

There is frequently found in churches a tendency for those who experience mental health difficulties to gather together to provide mutual support. Sometimes this occurs without anyone even realising that this is happening. At their best such relationships can be a source of comfort and encouragement because people have a shared experience. However, such relationships can sometimes prove to be emotionally draining for all involved, and run the risk of leaving you trying to support someone else emotionally when you yourself are feeling at a low ebb. When you are distressed yourself, it is sensible to reduce the amount that you see these friends for a time if you find that these emotional demands are difficult for you to deal with.

People who make unhelpful comments that add to your distress

Just as it is best to avoid a lot of contact with people who are themselves suffering from mental health problems when you are feeling depressed or anxious, the same is true for people who doggedly insist that *if only* you did this or that – had some particular ministry, confessed all sorts of sin, or had enough faith, or were more committed to God, or any number of other 'solutions' – you would soon be better.

Sadly in some churches, encouragement and support will not be the immediate response of some people including some leaders; their response may be to offer you some of the following solutions:

- Increase your church attendance.
- Increase your level of faith.

- Confess your sins, and possibly those of your parents, grandparents and great-grandparents.
- Seek deliverance from a curse or evil spirits.

We are not necessarily saying that all of these approaches are completely wrong or inappropriate, though in our experience they are often based on poor theology and a lack of understanding of mental health issues. We are concerned, however, that you receive the best support available from the Church, and the simple 'solutions' mentioned above are usually unhelpful.

You may also be directed to an organisation or individual that claims to 'specialise in ministry and/or deliverance for the mentally ill or disturbed'. Our advice would be to avoid such contact unless you are absolutely sure about the credentials of those involved; that it understands mental health issues well, and you feel completely comfortable with it. For a slightly fuller treatment of these issues you may find it useful to read the section on healing and deliverance in Chapter 10.

In order to improve how you feel, you will need people around you who will provide helpful support, and not those who, with the best intentions, have the effect of making you feel guilty or inadequate. Just as you would not dream of going to anyone other than a qualified medical practitioner to find out whether a lump or growth needed treatment, it is important that those whose advice you follow understand something of the nature and course of anxiety and depressive illnesses. While this does not include only those with qualifications in psychology or psychiatry, it is important that you have confidence in the qualifications or the experience of those offering advice.

In general terms God chooses to work through the local church, and has placed within most fellowships the gifts and ministries you need. Always seek support and prayer from the fellowship to which you belong first; they may not be perfect but they will usually be there for you the next time you need help.

In the great majority of cases you are likely to receive the positive support you need from your own fellowship, and we want to encourage you to remain as part of your local church if at all possible. If you are offered any form of ministry that is unhelpful, or if a church leader you speak to does not appear to react in a helpful way, what should you do? If you are able, try to persevere in explaining what you are experiencing; perhaps lend your leaders this book if you think they do not understand. Even so, there are occasions when church leaders and ministry teams do not handle mental health difficulties very well, and in spite of numerous attempts to explain the difficulty, the form of pastoral care and ministry you receive, or are offered, may only serve to make you feel worse. While this will be rare it does continue to happen occasionally, usually because of a lack of basic understanding from those offering pastoral care or prayer ministry or perhaps even an inability in them to cope with it themselves.

If this is the response you encounter, and things do not look as if they are going to alter, it may be best for you to prayerfully consider moving away for a time from the church you attend to another that is able to offer you more appropriate support and ministry. While this should be a last resort, if the form of ministry you receive, or are offered, adds to the difficulties you already encounter in overcoming depression or anxiety, you may have to face the fact that your current church has become part of the problem instead of part of the solution, and that remaining there will only make matters worse. Even if you do choose to try another church for a time, avoid losing all contact with your previous church.

What you can do to establish helpful relationships

Ensure that you have good relationships with people who value your friendship, people who resist making unrealistic demands on you, and affirm your worth and value to them as individuals and to the church of which you are a part.

Seek out Christian friends who can offer you:

- Loving support – people who are content simply to be with you and listen when you want to speak rather than offering easy solutions.

- Acceptance – of you for who you are.
- Sensible, practical advice when you ask for it.
- The space to make your own decisions.

If you can find just one Christian friend who will act in this way, and be prepared to stick with you for as long as it takes, allowing you to be yourself, then you will probably have found one of the major keys to your recovery.

A useful approach is to have pre-prepared a short one-line response to say to those people who you don't really know well (or who you don't wish to confide in) that you can use if they ask how you are. An example might be, 'I've been feeling really tired/washed out, but I'm getting through it now – thank you.' This answer is true, but avoids you getting drawn into conversations that you don't wish to take part in.

What if you yourself have a leadership role within your church?

If you have a position of responsibility or even leadership in your church, you may be afraid that your reputation will be damaged and your credibility as a leader undermined if you are feeling depressed or anxious. While this feeling is understandable, there is no reason why anyone should think any the less of you as a result. If we accept that mental illness, like physical illness, can happen to anyone at any time, there is no reason why it shouldn't also happen to you. Church leaders, clergy and lay alike, are in reality every bit as prone to depression and anxiety as anyone else, and responsibility in a Christian fellowship is no guarantee against these things occurring. Telling others in the church about your condition should really be no different from telling them that you have the flu or chicken pox.

Church responsibilities may well be an additional burden and source of difficulty if there are people or groups within the fellowship that depend on you to fulfil a particular role or perform a function. You may be a Sunday-school leader, part of a worship group or simply be responsible for making teas and coffees on a rota basis. Almost certainly you will feel an obligation to be there to 'do your bit' – even if the 'bit' is quite a lot. Others may exert pressure on you to keep performing a task, and you may be unwilling to drop out for fear of letting people down. If you are part of a small team where every available body counts, the pressure to keep doing your jobs can be almost overwhelming, and this may be worsened if you are someone who themselves has very high standards, and who is prone to take on too much responsibility for doing things (see Chapter 4, 'What are the causes of my anxiety and depression?').

Time after time people with leadership responsibilities try just to 'keep going' when they are experiencing anxiety or depression. This is an admirable desire, but in reality it is generally counterproductive, just as it would be to keep walking with a broken ankle. Instead of reducing their level of input into church life to match what they can manage, there is a grim determination not to give in, along with a belief that the problem will just pass. Sometimes it does, though the recovery process will almost always take longer this way. More often, though, the result of this gallant effort to keep going is that there is a 'crash'. The sufferer can no longer cope with anything, the work they were doing just comes to a grinding halt anyway, and the church then has two problems – the pastoral care of the person who is now really unwell, and how to arrange for their work to be covered by others. Thus you will really not have done yourself or your fellowship any favours by 'keeping going'.

What you can do if you are in a church leadership position and are finding it difficult to cope

It is almost always better to scale down what you do, whatever the response of those in your church fellowship. Give yourself the time and space needed to recover, and allow yourself the luxury of not wondering how the church will manage without you.

It is difficult to give definite rules about how much you should keep doing, since the extent of your depression or anxiety and your church roles and responsibilities will determine this. Perhaps the simplest approach is to see the depression or anxiety as you would any other illness; if you have a minor cold you may well feel able to carry on almost as normal, but if you have the flu you need to stop doing almost everything. The key is to pace what you do, as described in Chapter 7.

Just say 'no'

This can be quite difficult in church life, where every available worker often seems to be desperately needed, and pressure is frequently exerted to carry on no matter how you feel. Being able to assert yourself and just say 'no' is important in order to avoid ending up doing all sorts of jobs and performing multiple functions that have the effect of delaying your recovery, and possibly of even making you feel worse. Again a useful one-line statement that is truthful and polite, but firm, might be a good thing to prepare.

Summary

- Tell your church leaders in confidence how you feel.
- Seek out trustworthy Christian friends who will allow you to talk, pray for you, and support you in a helpful manner. Reduce or avoid dependent or critical relationships for the time being.
- Try to keep going to church, but consider going to fewer services if you are over-committed. Choose quieter services, arrive at the beginning and leave as soon as it has ended if this seems helpful.
- If you are in a leadership role, consider reducing what you do.
- As a last resort, find another church if you continue to receive a persistently unloving and unhelpful response.

CLOSING PRAYER

When you can, pray this prayer silently or preferably aloud.

Lord, thank you that you have placed me within a body of local believers. Please can you give me wisdom in what to say to them – show me who to confide in – help me to find those who can provide the best support.

Lord, sometimes I find it difficult praying, reading the Bible and going to church. Help me to reach the right balance of time spent with you both at home and also at church.

I pray also for all those others who are reading this book that they too will be able to find support and love from those around them within their own churches. I know that sometimes this support may not always be offered in the best ways, please particularly give wisdom to those in difficult situations so that they will know how best to respond.

Give grace, patience and wisdom to our church leaders and fellowship ministry teams.

Help me to seek out helpful relationships. Please give me the wisdom and grace to know if I need to cut down seeing anyone at the moment whose impact on me is unhelpful. Help me to do this in ways that don't hurt and upset these my friends.

Lord, thank you for your love, your forgiveness and your support.

Amen.

9

What about psychiatry and other mental health services?

So far in this book, you have looked at what depression and anxiety are (Chapters 1 and 2), how and why they can affect you (Chapters 3 and 4) and also considered different things you can do to overcome these difficulties (Chapters 5 to 8). However, sometimes depression and anxiety reach a level of severity where you may need to seek some additional help from a mental health professional. This chapter will help you to think about when to seek professional help, and provides an overview of the sorts of treatment that different health care practitioners can offer.

Acknowledging that there is a problem

You are probably reading this book because you yourself or someone you know is currently feeling depressed and/or anxious. When it comes to thinking about mental health problems such as these, the first important step is to acknowledge to ourselves that we have a problem.

It is often difficult to admit that we are feeling down and anxious and to acknowledge that we may have a depressive or anxiety illness. No one likes to see themselves as being mentally unwell. It's sometimes easier to try to keep going in the hope that the symptoms will pass with time. It is sometimes difficult to admit that we are struggling. Instead, we may prefer to put it all down to 'working too hard', 'feeling tired', or to blame 'a bug'. If a friend mentions to us that we are not managing or not looking well, we may take offence at this and decide that it is they who have the problem. It can be tempting to ignore the fact that we are becoming unwell: however, if we do the symptoms are unlikely to go away and the danger is that they may get worse. Ignoring the fact that we may be ill isn't a good idea.

Our belief is that the best approach to pastoral care for people with depression and anxiety or other psychiatric conditions is to see it in the same way as any physical illness. Depression and anxiety are not due to a lack of faith or a mistrust of God – they are illnesses and should be treated as such.

Example

Sometimes when a person feels depressed or anxious, they may say, 'I want to get better on my own.' But if the same person broke their leg, they wouldn't be saying that they want to get better on their own; instead they would want to go to hospital to have the bone set, have a plaster cast put on it and take antibiotics to ward off the risk of infection. Probably when a person makes that comment when depressed, it's because they have problems accepting that depression can be a serious condition.

Most people have an idea about treatments for physical illnesses: antibiotics for infection, insulin for diabetes or a plaster cast for a broken leg. Generally individuals are not so well-informed about the treatments that are available for depression and anxiety. Along with the stigma of mental illness, there are often preconceived ideas about mental health treatments with stereotyped fears that are inaccurate – tablets that make you feel like a 'zombie' or that are addictive, men in white coats forcing you into hospital against your will, and the use of hypnosis are all common stereotypes. The rest of this chapter will help you to find out more about the range of treatment options that are available.

Receiving help from the professionals

Imagine you live in a house that has a smoke detector. One day you hear it beeping while you are watching television. What do you do? Do you ignore it and keep watching the television as if there were no problem – or do you get up, find out if there is a problem and try to deal with it? If you are in a car and the low petrol warning light comes on, you know that if you ignore it you will run out of petrol. No matter how busy you are, you will stop and put petrol in the car. In the same way, if you notice any of the warning signs that depression or anxiety are starting to cause you problems, you need to do something to prevent the problem worsening.

If the problems begin to worsen in spite of your efforts to improve things, it is time to go to the professionals. If a fire is beginning to get out of control at home in spite of your attempts to tackle it, you would call the fire department for professional help. If you ran out of petrol you would call a garage or rescue service. In the same way, if you feel worse in spite of your attempts to overcome your difficulties, get in touch with your own health care practitioner or your doctor. They are there to help you and to advise you as to whether other additional approaches such as the use of medication may be helpful.

You are best advised to talk to your doctor when you recognise that you have symptoms of anxiety or depression. Don't wait for the symptoms to reach severe levels. In particular, you should always see your doctor if:

- You are feeling persistently low, or you have lost your ability to experience pleasure in things for a period of two weeks or more.
- You notice many negative thoughts about how you see yourself, your current situation or the future.
- You have started to significantly alter what you do because of how you feel – so that you have stopped doing many routine things, or

are starting to do things that are unhelpful and are adding to your problems such as drinking far more than normal or to excess.
- *Important note*: if you find that you are thinking a lot about suicide, or are beginning to make plans to harm or kill yourself or others, always see your doctor. Make this a priority.

YOUR GENERAL PRACTITIONER/PRIMARY CARE PHYSICIAN

Everyone has access to a community doctor such as general practitioner. If you aren't feeling well this is the best person to see first. Make an appointment and be prepared to be as honest as you can about how you feel. Pray and ask God for his help.

Before your appointment you may wish to spend a few minutes thinking and/or writing down the things you want to mention. You might want to include:

- What you see as the main problems.
- How long you have felt like this.
- Your symptoms (for example your emotions, physical changes, and your extreme thinking).
- Any practical or relationship difficulties that are part of the problem.
- What you have stopped doing as a result of how you feel.
- Any unhelpful behaviours, such as drinking, which you have started doing to cope with how you feel.

Take your notes along to the appointment. Don't be afraid to look at them during your appointment – they can give you confidence that you have covered all the main areas. If the initial appointment isn't long enough to do this, ask if you can come again for a longer appointment to talk through your concerns, or leave a copy of your list with your doctor for them to look at in their own time.

If you are anxious about the appointment, you may find it helpful to ask a friend to go with you. If you do this, decide beforehand if you wish your friend to go into the appointment with you, to sit in the waiting area with you or to wait outside for you. Be clear with your friend about what you would prefer.

Your doctor will no doubt ask a number of different questions as part of their assessment. These might include questions about how you feel and about your activities as well as your present circumstances and relationships. They may ask you specific questions relating to depression/anxiety, for instance about eating and sleep patterns, and if you have any thoughts of self-harm or suicide. They may ask questions that at first glance you may not realise are related to depression/anxiety. Your honest answers to these questions will help the doctor to make an accurate diagnosis and allow a suitable plan for your treatment to be put in place.

If you have had thoughts of suicide, it is important to talk about these. Don't be worried that by admitting to these you will be immediately admitted into hospital. Fleeting suicidal ideas are common in depression. Your doctor may ask for more details about these thoughts to make sure that you are offered the right level of support. This is particularly important if you are being increasingly troubled by such thoughts and are beginning to make plans to kill yourself. Surprisingly, talking about these thoughts may bring you some relief and reduce your anxiety.

Your doctor may also suggest that you have one or more blood tests. Don't be alarmed – this is to rule out the possibility of any underlying physical illnesses that may be worsening how you feel. Some physical illnesses can cause symptoms that are very similar to those of depression and anxiety; for example, some thyroid problems can produce a similar clinical picture to anxiety, and anaemia can produce low energy and make you feel tired all the time in a similar way to depression (see Chapter 4). It may take a couple of weeks for these blood test results to be processed and the results sent to your doctor.

Possible outcomes of seeing your doctor

Your doctor may ask you to come back to see them at a later date – possibly for a longer appointment. This will help provide a more thorough assessment. Your doctor may suggest you start taking an antidepressant or anti-anxiety medication (see below) and arrange to see you to review this in several weeks. In some instances, practices provide on-site access to counsellors or psychologists. Some practices may have a specialist nurse who will deal specifically with people who have problems with depression and anxiety.

Sometimes your doctor may suggest you take some time off work. If you are unwell you may not be able to function as well as usual at work and this may add to your stress. Taking time off work may be a difficult decision to make; it will depend on your symptoms and the type of work you do. If you have difficulty being around other people, you may find it is difficult when you have to work in a busy, noisy office, but you may manage if you work in quieter circumstances or on your own in a setting where you can pace yourself. Ideally if there is a colleague in whom you can confide, you could ask them for their opinion as to how you are managing. This has the advantage of providing an independent opinion rather than just relying on your own judgment which may be biased by your depression. Many organisations have good occupational health departments that will be able to see you confidentially and it can be worthwhile consulting them.

Referral to specialist workers or to voluntary sector organisations

Sometimes your doctor may suggest a referral to another professional or a voluntary support agency who can offer specific help. In the United Kingdom some possibilities are:

- Cruse – if your problem is due to bereavement. Contact Cruse Bereavement Care, Cruse House, 126 Sheen Road, Richmond, Surrey TW9 1UR; tel. 020 8940 4818; www.healthnetuk.com/new_site_3/cruse.htm
- Relate – if your problem is due to relationship difficulties. Tel. 01788 573241; www.relate.org.uk
- Citizens Advice Bureau for financial advice. Look at the National Association of Citizens Advice Bureau's website (www.nacab.org.uk) or use your local *Yellow Pages* to find a local branch.

- Occupational health – if your problem is due to work-related difficulties.
- Social services for difficulties of a social nature. Contact can be made through the *Yellow Pages*.
- Addiction services if there is a problem with alcohol or drugs. You can obtain details from your own doctor, or through *Yellow Pages*.

Another possibility is that your doctor may wish to refer you to a specialist mental health team.

WHAT IS A COMMUNITY MENTAL HEALTH TEAM?

In the United Kingdom mental health professionals often work together within a community mental health team. Generally the team is made up of a doctor (psychiatrist), who works with several community psychiatric nurses (CPNs), an occupational therapist (OT), a psychologist and a social worker.

All of these individuals work together to assess and plan an individual's care. Not every patient will need the full team to be involved in their care, and in many cases the individual may need to be seen by only one member of the team. If more than one member of the team is involved, in the United Kingdom, a care programme meeting will often take place at regular intervals. This is a joint meeting between yourself and the various health care practitioners you are seeing in order to make sure that everyone is clear about who is doing what, and that you agree with the treatment plan that is being offered. This can also be an opportunity to have relatives or carers present.

The following summarises the different practitioners who you may see if you are referred for specialist help. It is worth noting here that although the staff are called 'specialists', that shouldn't be interpreted as meaning that by seeing one of them you are such a complex case that you can only be helped by an expert. Instead, all the term 'specialist' means is that the person you see has received special training in the area of mental health.

What is a psychiatrist?

A psychiatrist is a doctor who has completed their usual medical training and then specialised in psychiatry, which is the branch of medicine that involves the assessment and treatment of mental health disorders. If you are referred to a psychiatrist you may see a doctor who is still in psychiatric training or a consultant who has completed their training. You may be seen in a general hospital, in a community clinic or sometimes at home. Most psychiatrists will use a combination of approaches – medication, social and psychological treatments – and may work with other colleagues – often within a community mental health team – to offer you help.

What is a community psychiatric nurse?

These are nurses who have trained specifically in mental health, have experience of working in a hospital setting but now work in the community. Some nurses will be trained in general nursing as well. Community psychiatric nurses can visit people at home to offer short-term counselling, support during bereavement, and short- or longer-term follow-up.

What is an occupational therapist?

Occupational therapists undergo general training and may then specialise in mental health. Occupational therapists look at the life skills an individual has and how well that individual is able to perform various activities (e.g. shopping and communicating with others). If you are finding it difficult at the moment coping or organising various life skills such as cooking or cleaning and this is causing you problems, the OT may be able to work with you to help you to overcome these problems and to encourage greater independence.

What is a clinical psychologist?

Psychology is a non-medical discipline concerned with the normal functioning of the mind in areas such as learning and remembering. Clinical psychologists complete a psychology degree at university and then go on to do further training in mental health difficulties.

The treatment that is offered is usually one of a number of psychological or 'talking' therapies. Psychologists are not doctors and therefore do not prescribe medication.

What is a mental health social worker?

Social workers complete a general training in social work and may then specialise in mental health. They assess social needs such as housing and finance and have particular knowledge about how this applies to those with mental health problems. Within the United Kingdom, some social workers may do further training and become 'approved social workers'. This means that they are able to carry out certain roles as determined by the Mental Health Act.

What is a psychotherapist?

There are different types of psychotherapy (see later) and so psychotherapists tend to come from a variety of professional backgrounds. They have trained in a particular branch of psychotherapy. Within the UK at the moment there is no central professional body regulating the practice of psychotherapy, unlike the other professions mentioned here. This means that anyone can legally call themselves a psychotherapist. It is important to ensure that any psychotherapist you see has received adequate initial training, is committed to continuing training, and receives regular clinical supervision. In the UK, this is normally shown by the person being accredited by a nationally recognised organisation such as the British Association for Behavioural and Cognitive Psychotherapies (BABCP, www.babcp.com; Tel. 01254 875277). BABCP is the lead organisation for Cognitive Behavioural Therapy in the UK and will be able to provide the names and contact details of CBT practitioners who work within the NHS or privately in different parts of the country. If you wish to use another form of psychotherapy, a useful contact point to identify accredited practitioners is the United Kingdom Council for Psychotherapy (UKCP, www.psychotherapy.org.uk; Tel. 020 7436 3002).

WHAT HAPPENS WHEN YOU ARE REFERRED TO A MENTAL HEALTH SPECIALIST?

The initial assessment

Your own doctor will normally organise an appointment with the mental health practitioner. This will take place either in a local hospital, a local community health centre or may even be at your own home. Usually the first appointment lasts for about an hour, although follow-up appointments – if they are offered – are often for shorter periods.

Take with you any medication you have been prescribed. You may wish to ask a friend to go with you. Again you may wish your friend to wait in the car for you, to sit in the waiting area or to go into the appointment with you. Be clear about what you want. If they do go in with you be aware that having them there may help boost your confidence. Their presence, however, may make you more reluctant to talk about some of the problems you face since you may not want them to hear all of what you say.

You are likely to be asked about how you feel in detail and also about your past including your childhood, schooling and employment as well as information about your family, medical history and past mental health problems. These are all routine questions, which are designed to provide as much information as possible about you. This allows the psychiatrist or team member to decide what is wrong with you and how you can best be treated. You may be asked about previous and current relationships including questions about difficulties in any current sexual relationships. This is asked because sexual difficulties are often not mentioned spontaneously by people but can be present. If you find these particular questions intrusive, just say that you would prefer not to talk about those issues. If you do have problems in this area (which is often the case in anxiety and depression), we recommend that you just say so. The practitioner will have spoken to many people who have similar problems; they won't be shocked by your answers and will try to help you with any difficulties.

At the end of the initial assessment, the treatment options will be discussed with you. If there is anything you are uncertain about just ask so that you can understand what is offered. Write the options down if you think you may have problems remembering what is said (or the practitioner may be able to offer you information leaflets summarising many of the main treatment options – ask if these are available).

WHAT TREATMENTS ARE AVAILABLE FOR ANXIETY AND DEPRESSION?

A wide range of physical (e.g. treatment with tablets), psychological (treatment by talking) and social treatments (e.g. help with debts and relationships) are available, and the key is agreeing on the right mix to meet the needs of each individual. The following is a broad outline of the types of treatment that may be offered. This is not an exhaustive list nor are any dealt with in great detail, but hopefully it will give you an overview of what is available.

PHYSICAL TREATMENT

Antidepressant medication

Antidepressants are designed to combat depression. When individuals are depressed, certain chemicals (called neurotransmitters) within the brain drop to a lower level than normal. The main two neurotransmitters are noradrenaline and serotonin. Antidepressants increase these neurotransmitters back to their normal levels and so treat the symptoms of depression.

Many antidepressants have some anti-anxiety properties and can also treat anxiety, either when this is the main problem, or when the person has mixed symptoms of anxiety and depression. This can explain why sometimes an antidepressant can be prescribed when in fact the main problem is anxiety.

Currently the three most used chemical groups of antidepressant are:

- The tricyclic antidepressants.
- The selective serotonin re-uptake inhibitors (SSRIs).
- The serotonin noradrenaline re-uptake inhibitors (SNRIs).

Other tablet groups also exist such as the mono-amine oxidase inhibitors, but are generally less used than the above three groups of tablets. All are effective at treating depression. You may find that a particular practitioner may have a preference for one or other type of medication based on their own experience and familiarity with it.

Antidepressants can be an important part of treating all aspects of depression. Because there are links between the altered thinking, feelings, behaviour and physical aspects of depression, the physical treatment offered by an antidepressant can lead to positive improvements in unhelpful and extreme thinking, low mood and unhelpfully altered behaviour.

Who do antidepressants work best for?

Antidepressants are most often helpful when one or more of the following are present:

- Significant depression (low mood and a lack of enjoyment).
- Several of the physical changes of depression (e.g. low energy, reduced concentration, altered sleep or appetite).
- Significant agitation or the onset or worsening of suspiciousness or panic.
- Suicidal ideas: where you can't see a future.

How long do they take to work?

Normally, antidepressants take about ten to fourteen days to begin to work and their positive actions may take up to four to six weeks to reach a peak. It is very important, therefore, to take the tablets regularly and for long enough, even if to begin with they might seem not to be working. Overall, around two-thirds of patients respond to the first antidepressant medication they are prescribed. If there is little or no improvement, often an increase in dose or a change of medication will effectively treat the depression.

Warning A common problem is that the person stops the antidepressants when they first feel well again. Stopping an antidepressant too early is a common cause of worsening depression. It is usually necessary to take the antidepressant medication for about six to nine months after feeling better to prevent slipping back into depression.

Do antidepressants have side effects?
All tablets have side effects. The important question is what is worse – having side effects or having untreated depression/anxiety. Many side effects disappear within a few days of starting the tablets as the body becomes used to them. Antidepressants aren't addictive. However, if a person has taken the tablets at a high dose for some time it is sensible for the dose of the antidepressant to be reduced slowly over a number of days before being stopped. Modern antidepressants are often not very sedating and don't cause very great weight gain.

Antidepressants are the fastest and most effective way of improving depression in the short term, especially if certain symptoms are present. If you are feeling very depressed, they can help you reach a stage where you are able to look at making changes in your life to help prevent the depression occurring again. If you are taking an antidepressant, or wish to discuss whether taking one is likely to be helpful for you, you should do so with your doctor. Speak to your doctor about the best treatment for your illness. Remember, it is unwise to stop taking antidepressants without the agreement of your doctor.

What about drinking alcohol when I also take antidepressants?
We recognise that there is a range of Christian opinion about whether it is wise to drink alcohol at all. If you do drink, you need to be particularly careful when taking antidepressants because sometimes taking medication with alcohol can make people feel very drowsy. Therefore it's best to avoid or limit alcohol if you are taking antidepressants.

What about driving?

Some antidepressants can impair concentration and alertness and therefore driving. Read and follow the advice issued with your medication. If there is any doubt, don't drive and discuss this with your doctor.

What about pregnancy?

Generally most drugs pass through the placenta to the developing baby. Some antidepressants are safe to take during pregnancy and some are not. For most of the antidepressants there is insufficient evidence to say if they are safe or not. For this reason, it is generally best to avoid medication during pregnancy, and in particular during the first three months of pregnancy when the development of the baby can be most affected. If you are on medication and become pregnant, consult your doctor as soon as possible.

What about breast-feeding?

Many antidepressants will pass to the baby through breast milk. For many of the drugs, the amount passed is very small and will not be a reason to not breast-feed. However, this is an area you should speak to your doctor about.

My attitudes towards antidepressants

Antidepressant medications are sometimes viewed with suspicion, particularly by some sections of the Church. The following questions address some commonly held concerns about antidepressant medication.

Antidepressants are addictive

Useful information

It isn't possible to become addicted to modern antidepressants in the same way as to alcohol or tablets like diazepam. Antidepressants do need to be taken sensibly and as recommended by your doctor. If tablets are started at too high an initial dose, side effects are more common; similarly if a tablet taken at a high dose is stopped suddenly, some short-lived discontinuation symptoms may occur. To prevent this, many tablets are first started by slowly increasing the dose, and then later stopped by tapering down their dose over several days.

I should get better on my own without taking tablets
Antidepressants are often one of a number of ways of getting better. They work by treating some of the physical changes that occur in depression by increasing noradrenaline and serotonin levels back towards normal. They don't replace the need for you to identify and work at changing extreme or unhelpful thoughts and behaviours or the different practical problems you face. They can, however, be a useful additional way of improving how you feel. If your doctor is recommending antidepressants, talk to them and discuss why they suggest this so that you can jointly make the decision about whether this is the right thing for you at the moment.

They cause side effects
All tablets cause side effects. The question is whether the benefits of taking the tablets outweigh the costs. Often side effects diminish over the first few days of taking an antidepressant. Sometimes the dose of antidepressant can be reduced, or a different antidepressant with a different range of side effects can be prescribed.

Mood stabilisers

There are some types of medication called 'mood stabilisers'. These are designed, as their name suggests, to stabilise mood. The main two are lithium and carbamazepine. They tend to be used by people who have recurrent episodes of depression, or of very high mood – mania or hypomania – or of alternating high and low mood. This group of clinical disorders are called 'bipolar disorders'. They are also used in those with chronic depression or severe, recurrent depression. They can be used in combination with other antidepressants.

The most commonly used mood stabiliser is lithium, which is a type of salt that can be found naturally. The kidneys excrete it and so these need to be working well for lithium to be used. The doctor will monitor the level of lithium in the blood to make sure that the dose used is high enough to be effective, but not so high that it causes unpleasant and potentially dangerous side effects (as seen in lithium toxicity). Instructions on how to identify this and what to do if it is present can be found on the information you receive with the medication.

Other types of medication sometimes used in depression and anxiety include:

Antipsychotic medication

Antipsychotic medication (also called major tranquillisers) is more usually used to treat illnesses such as schizophrenia, but can also be prescribed for other disorders such as anxiety and depression. At smaller doses they are effective in the treatment of anxiety or agitation and also reduce the fearful thoughts seen in more severe forms of depression.

Benzodiazepines

Benzodiazepines (also called minor tranquillisers, anxiolytics, hypnotic or sleeping tablets) help treat both anxiety and sleeplessness. Benzodiazepines are not a cure for anxiety or sleeplessness but only alleviate the symptoms. Benzodiazepine medication should usually be prescribed for only short periods of time – usually no more than a few weeks. A problem that can occur is that if taken for too long they can cause tolerance (where increasingly higher doses are needed to obtain an effect), and dependency with withdrawal symptoms occurring in many cases if they are prescribed beyond the recommended time. It is probably better to look at other ways of dealing with sleeplessness or anxiety rather than using this type of medication.

What about alternative medicine and herbal remedies?

Many people are now trying alternate therapies or herbal remedies before embarking on the more traditional methods of treating depression. There may be a place for this in the milder forms of depression and anxiety, but herbal remedies can also have side effects and may interact with other medication prescribed by your doctor.

One commonly used herb is St John's Wort (hypericum perforatum). This is used a lot in Germany and claims have been made that it is an effective antidepressant for those with a mild to moderate illness. No research has been completed examining its long-term use, however, and it can also interact with prescribed medication so in general if you are considering alternative therapies:

- Don't start any herbal remedies before consulting your doctor.
- Don't stop your prescribed medication until you have spoken to your doctor.

Choice point

If you are taking antidepressants at the moment, the following section is designed to help you to use them most effectively. If you are not taking tablets, then please skip this section and move to page 227, where another treatment for depression – electroconvulsive therapy – is described.

Optional section: using antidepressants effectively

Remembering to take antidepressants

For almost any medication, it may be difficult to remember to take them on a regular basis. This is particularly the case in depression because of the poor concentration and forgetfulness that can often occur.

Q. Do you sometimes forget to take your medication?
Yes ❑ No ❑

Helpful hints
The following may help you to remember to take your tablets:

- Get into a routine: take the tablets at a set time each day.
- Place the tablets somewhere where you will see them when you get up or go to bed (e.g. by your toothbrush).
- Write little notes to yourself saying 'Medication' (or any other word to help remind you if you don't want others to read them). Think about your routine and what you will be doing at the time of day when you need to take the tablets. Stick little notes on places that you will see such as on the fridge door, the television, oven or back door so that you are reminded throughout the day.

Important point Please always make sure that children can never obtain access to your tablets. Accidental overdoses can occur, and it would be a tragic accident if something that was supposed to help actually ended up causing harm.

Q. Do you ever get confused as to whether you have taken the medication? Yes ❑ No ❑

Helpful hints
The following may help you be clear when you have taken your medication:

- Tick off the doses you have taken in a diary or calendar.
- If you are taking lots of tablets at different times each day, a dosette box can help. These have different compartments for each time of day so that you, or a friend, neighbour or health care practitioner can fill the box up in advance for the whole week. Ask your health care practitioner or pharmacist how to get one.

Q. Do you ever take a higher dose than is prescribed?
Yes ❑ No ❑

Key point: It is very important not to take a higher dose of antidepressant than your doctor prescribes. Antidepressant tablets work over a number of weeks. Taking more on one particular day will have no impact on your depression. It is the constant taking of them day in and day out at the correct dose that will lead to improvement. Tablets taken at higher than recommended doses may cause unpleasant side effects, or even be dangerous. If you are concerned that an antidepressant is not working (remember they take at least two weeks to begin to work), please discuss this with your doctor.

What about electroconvulsive therapy?

Over the last few decades the frequency with which electroconvulsive therapy (ECT) has been offered has dropped dramatically. It is now offered in only relatively few cases. This bears testimony to the effectiveness of other treatments such as the newer antidepressants, and the development of accessible and effective psychological treatments.

ECT is a recognised and effective treatment for depression, but tends now to be mainly used for cases of treatment resistant or life-threatening depression. It is particularly useful when there is difficulty with side effects from medication, when someone is highly agitated or suicidal, or if a person isn't eating or drinking because of their symptoms of depression. ECT has a particularly bad public image as portrayed sometimes in films and the media. In reality, much that is shown there is ill-informed. If your doctor is suggesting this as a treatment possibility we suggest you talk to them and other practitioners, and also ask if you can speak to people who have had ECT themselves in order to find out more about the advantages and disadvantages of this treatment. Some patients who have recurrent depression will request ECT since it has worked so well for them in the past.

In reality, electroconvulsive therapy involves the passage of a small electrical stimulus to the brain for a short period of time. This then produces an epileptic fit. The dose is adjusted so that a patient receives the smallest amount of electrical current that is needed to produce a seizure. In the UK, ECT is highly regulated by central bodies and is given only by staff who have been trained in its administration and in units that are equipped to perform this. Because the person is often drowsy for a few hours after the treatment, it is offered largely to inpatients. In the UK it is given under the guidance of a psychiatrist and in the presence of an anaesthetist. The procedure is explained to the patient beforehand and only given with their written consent, except in special circumstances under the regulations of the Mental Health Act. The person first receives a muscle relaxant and a sedative. The ECT is then given and the time of the fit is measured. Patients then recover in the same way as they would from any general anaesthetic before returning to the ward. The number of treatments required varies from person to person depending on the severity of the illness and the response to treatment. It is usually given twice a week.

PSYCHOLOGICAL AND SOCIAL TREATMENTS

There are a variety of psychological (talking) therapies that offer effective treatment for depression and anxiety. A recent document published by the Department of Health (DoH 2001) summarises which psychological therapies are effective treatments for common mental health problems such as anxiety and depression. A few that are currently available in the UK are mentioned below. The aim of these treatments is to improve symptoms, overcome relationship difficulties and generally improve day-to-day functioning.

People can choose individual or group therapy. In individual therapy the individual will work only with the therapist/practitioner; in group therapy, the individual will take part in treatment sessions with one or two therapists/practitioners and also a number of other people who share the same sorts of clinical problems.

Cognitive Behaviour Therapy

The Department of Health report shows that Cognitive Behaviour Therapy (CBT) has the strongest evidence base as an effective treatment for anxiety, panic and depression. This current book is based on CBT principles. CBT involves helping the person look at their own thought processes and behaviour. How we think affects how we feel and behave, and what we do. Treatment using CBT involves identifying and then challenging extreme and unhelpful thoughts, and planning out ways to overcome reduced activity and unhelpful behaviour that may be a part of depression. It does this by asking people questions and providing important information to try to help the person to make changes to improve how they feel. CBT treatments can be offered on an individual or group basis, and also through self-help books such as this one. A strong evidence base now suggests that CBT principles can be effectively taught through self-help books and this may be particularly helpful for problems such as anxiety and depression.

Psychodynamic and psychoanalytic therapies

These forms of therapy have developed from psychoanalytical theory, which has its roots in the work of Freud. In this approach the therapist tries to identify unhelpful patterns of behaviour that occur, and link these to unconscious defence mechanisms that the person repeatedly uses in their relationships with others. The person's present thoughts and behaviour are seen as being based on early and often damaging past experiences. By examining the past, the individual is able to make changes in the here and now and thus resolve their symptoms of anxiety and depression. Different types of psychotherapy last for variable amounts of time and traditionally have been offered as longer-term treatments for an hour a week for over a year. In recent times, briefer forms of psychodynamic therapy have been developed and these have been shown to be effective.

Counselling

This is a form of treatment that gives the person an opportunity to look at how they live and discover new ways of living and coping for the future. The focus of the counselling may be specific such as marital counselling for relationship difficulties, or bereavement counselling when the main problem has been an issue of loss.

Relaxation techniques

A range of relaxation techniques can sometimes be of help particularly when problems of physical tension are a large part of the problem. Most involve the progressive relaxation of different muscles in the body. In many cases of anxiety, over-breathing (sometimes called 'hyperventilation') occurs, so many forms of relaxation aim to help to control breathing. Most large bookshops sell a range of relaxation tapes or videotapes, some of which are better than others.

The really good thing about learning a relaxation technique is that it is you who is learning this new skill. Once you have acquired the skill of controlling anxiety, this skill is then yours for life. The approach isn't devised to be used alone when anxiety is present. Instead, it can be added to other work you are doing to help identify and challenge the unhelpful and extreme fears and altered behaviour that are acting to maintain your symptoms of anxiety.

Problem solving

This is a step-by-step way of identifying and then tackling specific practical problems that you face. You can read more about how to use the problem solving approach within Chapter 7 of this book.

SUMMARY

A range of health care practitioners exists, with specialist training and skills in mental health disorders.

- Mental health practitioners include psychiatrists, clinical psychologists, occupational therapists, nursing staff and social workers.

- Sometimes it can be sensible to see a professional – particularly if things just seem to be getting worse, and you have noticed that the feelings of anxiety or depression are affecting you badly, dominating how you feel or think and causing you to significantly alter what you do.
- *Always* go to see someone if you begin to have suicidal thoughts or find yourself becoming hopeless.
- If you have been very depressed or anxious before, and you begin to notice similar symptoms returning – go and see someone at an early stage to discuss what can be done now to prevent the symptoms worsening.

Antidepressants may have an important role in helping people with anxiety and depression to recover.

- Antidepressants are an effective treatment for many people with depression, and some can effectively also treat anxiety and panic symptoms as well.
- Antidepressants are safe to take at their prescribed dosages if you follow the instructions given by your doctor, who will explain the amount of medication to take and when. The medicine bottle or packet will also have these instructions on it.
- Antidepressants aren't addictive, but in stopping higher doses it is sensible to slowly reduce the amount taken over a period of time in liaison with your doctor.
- Taking the tablets on a regular basis is essential for them to work. If you are taking tablets, use the techniques described in this chapter to help you to take them more reliably.
- All tablets have side effects, but for most people the benefits of antidepressants far outweigh the costs.

Certain psychological treatments such as Cognitive Behaviour Therapy (CBT) have a proven effectiveness in the treatment of anxiety and depression, and this can be accessed through individual or group treatments, or by using self-help materials.

CLOSING PRAYER

When you can, pray this prayer silently or preferably aloud.

Dear Father,
Having read this chapter, I think of my own life and how I have been feeling. If it is time for me to seek help, then help me to do this. Give me the strength to go to my doctor about this and to speak to them. Give me the words to say and the courage to be honest. It is difficult to ask for this help and I ask that you would be with me in this.

I pray for others reading this book that they may consider whether they need professional help. If so, grant them the ability to seek and to accept the help given.

I also think of all those people in the mental health care professions and I thank you for them. Thank you especially for Christians who are health care professionals. Thank you for calling them into that work, and I pray particularly for any that I know. I pray that you may give them wisdom in the work that they do, guide them in the decisions they make and allow their skill to be used as part of your healing process.

Amen.

REFERENCES

Department of Health (2001), *Treatment Choice in Psychological Therapies and Counselling: Evidence Based Clinical Practice Guideline Brief Version*, Department of Health: London.
A short summary is available for download from: www.doh.gov.uk/mentalhealth/treatmentguideline

PART 4:
PRACTICAL HELP FOR CHURCH LEADERS

10

Practical help for church leaders – how the Church can help and how sometimes it doesn't

'You're either part of the solution or you're part of the problem.'
(Eldridge Cleaver, American political activist, 1968)

The Church can be a tremendous asset to those who are distressed. This final chapter is written especially for church leaders or pastoral team members, and will be of interest to other Christians who find themselves in the position of supporting fellow church members who are depressed or anxious. While this book is generally concerned with anxiety and depression, much of the material in this chapter is equally appropriate for ministry to people with almost any psychiatric disorder. Our challenge within the Church is how to offer something effective, and to do so with credibility.

OFFERING A UNIFIED APPROACH

Mental health is a problem area for many Christians in a way that isn't true of any other branch of medicine. Mental health care practitioners are frequently suspicious of those who minister in the name of religion – and often not without reason – while many church leaders think that psychiatric treatment can often ignore important aspects of human experience such as spiritual issues. In contrast, perhaps a more helpful approach is to acknowledge that both spiritual and medical approaches can be helpful aspects of whole-person care. Increasingly within the UK and the USA, spiritual aspects of care are seen as important, and this is reflected in the recent formation of a religion and spirituality special interest group within the main professional body for psychiatrists within the UK – the Royal College of Psychiatrists.

GIVING THE RIGHT MESSAGE

The process of offering effective support to distressed people who come to our churches starts well before we recognise that they have mental health problems. For our churches to be really effective in supporting those with mental health difficulties, we need to establish a culture where everyone in the local church knows that it is acceptable to have problems from time to time, and that the church as a whole – and especially its leadership – is there to support church members during these times as well as in times of success. Ideally this work in agenda-setting needs to begin quite some time before an individual develops mental illness rather than as a response to it.

In this realm of agenda-setting there are three particular concerns to highlight:

Overcoming the stigma of mental illness

Research has shown that for every person who presents with mental health difficulties to their physician, there is another who doesn't. This is often because people are afraid of the stigma they associate with mental health problems. Mental illness in our society has a serious image problem. Sometimes mental health hospitals are sadly described by a minority as 'loony bins', and those who are admitted there are labelled as 'mad'. In fact the sort of people who decide to seek out psychiatric treatment are ordinary people who just happen to be experiencing various mental health problems. Indeed, almost anyone can experience mental health problems, given the wrong sequence of life experiences and stressors.

The same unhelpful attitudes can also sometimes be found even within our churches. In order to begin to overcome the stigma and prejudice that often accompanies mental health problems, you and your church must clearly state that:

- Church members do not have to be 'perfect' – never experiencing any problems. Make it clear that the Church will and does offer love and support to those who are distressed.
- The Christian life can be difficult and challenging at times as well as having times of peace and joy. This is shown in the life of Jesus, the apostles and countless other Christians over the centuries. Being a Christian does not automatically protect us from life's difficulties (Chapter 1), and for many, a new set of problems starts when they become Christians. It is important to present a full and accurate picture of what life – even as a Christian believer – is really like. The book of Psalms addresses just about every imaginable element in the life of the believer and every emotion God's people are likely to experience. It is therefore instructive that between a quarter and a third of the psalms deal with themes such as oppression, fear and despair. It seems not unreasonable that a balanced diet of our teaching, pastoring and Bible study should reflect this picture.
- You and your church offer love and support for all – in particular this means that it is made clear that you do not withdraw when people develop life problems, and that you do not favour those in the church who are seen as more attractive and/or successful (James 2:1–9).

- There is a willingness to be open and honest with each other when in difficulty. For example an ability to say to someone 'I know you are very upset, and I'm not sure quite what to say, but I'm here to support you in any way you might find helpful.'
- Confidentiality is respected when asked for. This issue of trust is discussed in greater detail with reference to pastoral teams later in this chapter.

These principles need to become part of the long-term way of working and teaching within the Church. These values can be clearly and explicitly stated, and also implicitly reinforced in the attitudes communicated in sermons, Bible studies and prayers. This can be done in our choice of topics, biblical passages for teaching and preaching, selection of material for worship and in small groups and in providing a variety of worship that includes the reflective and contemplative elements of faith as well as the joyful and exuberant. Overall, a clear statement should be made that an important part of the ministry of the local church is to support the body of believers who attend it as they are now – warts and all.

Be prepared to be misunderstood

Part of being anxious and depressed means that the person may find it difficult to seek help. This can be because of negative views of how the person sees themselves, their current situation and the future. The person may often be very sensitive to perceived criticism and become very aware of how they are being judged by others. Mind-reading occurs where the person may second-guess that others don't like them or are rejecting them. This can create potential difficulties when it comes to us trying to offer supportive help. Because it isn't possible to always get things right, or offer unlimited input, and because of the possibility that things that we say (or don't say) may be interpreted as personal criticism, the danger is that the person we are trying to support may become hurt or angry. The understandable reaction is for them to either hit back (verbally rather than physically in most cases) or to avoid us, and go away. Wisdom, humility and judgment is therefore required. We need to anticipate that this situation may arise and plan out how we can respond effectively if it does.

Establishing some ground rules in the relationship can be helpful:

- Say at the outset that you are there to help, but that you may sometimes misunderstand things or get things wrong. Agree that you will always be honest in what you say.
- Encourage the person to say if they are annoyed or upset by anything you say or do.
- Apologise when you get things wrong.
- Ask for a chance to clarify what you mean when there is a chance of misunderstanding.
- A useful hint is to look for obvious changes in how the person looks as you talk to them. If they suddenly appear annoyed or more upset, ask yourself, 'What could be going through their mind right now? Could anything I have said have been misinterpreted or caused a problem?' This offers you the chance to clarify what has been said and to correct any problems.

Don't think that you have to have all the answers

Sometimes as people, we all want to provide the answer to a person's problem. For members of pastoral or ministry teams the desire to 'sort things out' is often fairly strong, and when we are ministering to Christians experiencing depression or anxiety we may well have to face up to the reality of there not being an immediate and easy solution. The temptation we may face in such a setting is to try to say or do something that will make things better immediately, or else search for a possible cause of the problem that can be rectified.

It is important to say to those who we seek to help with depression and anxiety that we do not have quick fixes or easy solutions. A far more honest – and helpful – approach may be to say something like this: 'I would love to be able to do or say something to make you feel better and change the way you see things right now, but to be honest I don't know what the answer is. But I'd like to keep praying for you and listening to you, and spend time sharing with you until you are feeling better than you are now.'

EXAMINING YOUR PERSONAL AND CHURCH ATTITUDES

One of the most helpful things you can do if you are ministering to people with anxiety or depression is to ask yourself some basic questions about who you are, how you see people who are distressed, and in particular why you are involved in the business of caring for people with mental health difficulties.

Your personal attitudes

Because what you think can affect how you feel and what you do, it is important to be aware of your own immediate thoughts when working with those who are distressed. These attitudes will affect the way in which we offer support to those who are distressed within the Church. The following questions will help you to consider your own and your church's attitudes and reactions towards mental health problems. It may be tempting to answer these questions quite quickly with what you perceive as the 'correct' answer, so it is really important to choose to allow yourself to really reflect on the questions.

You may find it useful to stop and pray at this point, before answering these questions. The purpose isn't to make you feel bad about yourself as a Christian leader or church member, but instead to help you to begin to think about things that may need to change for you to be even more effective in providing support for others.

How much do I personally see the emotional/feeling side of faith as being important?

Think about your own attitudes towards styles of worship and towards relating to God in private and in church. How much do I depend for my own spiritual security on being able to 'feel' God's love and how much is this an academic/intellectual issue for me? Consider where you are on the scale of head and heart orientation.

Q. Am I head- or heart-orientated?

Q. How does this affect how I relate to believers experiencing depression or anxiety who are at a different point on the scale from me?

Q. How might these factors affect the advice I might give to such people?

What factors have shaped my attitudes and responses towards mental health problems?

Think about the historical factors (upbringing, childhood memories of illness, comments that parents have made) that may affect how you approach mental illness.

Q. How has my own upbringing affected my view of the origin of mental health problems?

Q. Where did I learn these attitudes from? What informed the development of these beliefs?

Now consider your reactions to Christians who are anxious or depressed. It may help to think back to one or two encounters you have found difficult. How do these historical factors affect your reaction now towards Christian believers who are experiencing depression or anxiety?

Q. Do I regularly feel uncomfortable when speaking to distressed people, and if so what could explain that feeling?

Q. Do I try to avoid speaking to people suffering from any form of mental illness, and if so why does this happen?

Q. Think about the messages that you are sending out to people in distress. What helpful and unhelpful signals do I send out?

Q. How can I make it clearer that I want to offer appropriate support and help?

Who holds the power?

An issue that is always present in any ministering relationship is that of power – the balance of the relationship between the person who is distressed and the person who is offering support. We suggest that our approach should generally be to allow the sufferer to set the agenda. Sometimes this doesn't happen, and when this is the case, we may have to ask why. Do we have the wrong motives for helping those who are anxious or depressed?

Ask yourself the following questions:

- Do I regularly find myself seeking out people who need help?
- Is this primarily because I desire to meet their needs or my own?
- Do I continually feel the need to 'solve their problem'?
- Do I frequently try to find spiritual explanations for someone's mental illness?
- Am I ever judgmental, jumping to conclusions about why someone is experiencing such difficulties?

One of the most difficult things we may have to face in supporting people with mental illness is that sometimes we are motivated more by our needs than by theirs. Hopefully the above questions will help you see to what extent this may be true for you. If you found yourself consistently answering 'yes' to the above questions you may need to ask yourself some hard questions about what you are doing and why you are doing it. This does not mean that you should forget about caring for those experiencing difficulties like depression and anxiety, but it may be time to reflect on your motivation, and perhaps find someone you can talk to about your approach to caring for people with mental illness.

Church attitudes

This section has been difficult to write, and we are aware that we are in something of a minefield here because we are addressing deeply ingrained attitudes about how we see God, fellow Christians and the spiritual aspects of depression and anxiety. Readers are likely to vary in their own beliefs about the relationship of mental health difficulties to the personal faith of the sufferer.

Task

To begin with, think about your own individual church background. Are any of the following statements made in your fellowship?

- Mental illness is mainly caused by insufficient faith, inadequate commitment, personal sin or disobedience to God.
- Most mental illnesses, particularly depression and schizophrenia, are due to demonic activity.
- Greater levels of faith and claiming victory would result in healing and/or deliverance.
- There is an inherited 'root' in the family history that has been passed on through generations that is causing poor mental health.

Later on in this chapter we will think specifically about the issues of healing and deliverance, but for the present think about the effect these statements are likely to have on people experiencing depression or anxiety.

Think about the following:

- What would the impact be on me if I was depressed and I was told that this was because of my own sin?
- What would the impact be on me if I was anxious and I was told that this was because of my lack of faith?
- What would the impact be on me if I was distressed and I was told that this was because of the work of the devil within me?

Since the sufferer is already likely to be experiencing significant levels of guilt and worthlessness these statements may add to their despair and condemnation.

- They will be given a 'diagnosis' but possibly no programme of treatment. Frequently such statements are made in a vacuum, and the sufferer is left to work it out for themself.

- If the ministry that is carried out on the basis of this analysis yields little tangible improvement almost inevitably the blame for this failure will revert to the person who is depressed or anxious, thus deepening the spiral of guilt and worthlessness.

Of course it is true that people who are experiencing depression, anxiety and other mental illness may sometimes have made choices that have worsened their own situations. Since our goal must always be the restoration of the individual to normal health, however, our belief is that these kind of global statements are counterproductive, as well as usually being untrue.

Our concern in raising these issues is that sometimes such strong statements are made for the benefit of the person making them, rather than the benefit of the sufferer.

- Sometimes they arise from a fundamental lack of understanding about the causes and nature of mental illness.
- Such statements allow the person making them to avoid drawing alongside the sufferer.
- Sometimes the person making the statement holds strong views about which they are actually rather insecure. If someone does not fit into the expected framework, and continues to suffer from poor mental health, an explanation has to be found that does not undermine the beliefs that are so dearly held. This usually involves placing the blame for any failure on the person who is suffering from poor mental health. Needless to say, this just makes matters worse.

In writing these things we are aware that there are a range of views about the relationship between demonic forces, past and present sin and mental health issues, and something of our understanding of these issues can be found in the section on healing and deliverance. The point we want to emphasise here, however, is that the paramount concern should always be for the wellbeing of the person who is unwell, and that they should be held in a supportive and understanding framework of care. This will ensure that the person who is unwell is empowered and, where possible, sets the agenda according to their needs rather than those of the person offering the ministry.

If possible, please read through this section on personal and church attitudes again, reflect once more on the answers to the questions we raise, and seek to be completely honest with yourself. We hope that such an approach will assist you and your fellowship in becoming more effective in caring for people with depression, anxiety or another form of mental illness.

THINGS YOU CAN DO TO ENCOURAGE DISCUSSION OF EMOTIONAL ISSUES

A well-known quote from the 1960s is that 'You're either part of the solution or you're part of the problem' (Eldridge Cleaver, American political activist, 1968). Our purpose here is to offer some practical as well as theoretical guidelines that may help you in the work of supporting someone who is experiencing depression or anxiety. We want to begin with a short Bible study of the first few chapters of the book of Job, and it may be useful at this point if you have a Bible with you.

Many people think of the book of Job as a contribution to the debate about innocent suffering, and indeed it is that, but it has much else to offer too. The early chapters are a good example of how to help, and how not to help, someone experiencing distress.

Job had every reason to feel depressed – and anxious. A man of immense wealth and influence, with a strong faith in God and the head of a large and apparently happy family, he rapidly lost almost everything that was important to him – his property, his livelihood and his children, and all for reasons that were unknown to him at the time. He was understandably depressed when three of his friends came to visit him (Job 2:11–13). These friends started off really well because of their motive and their actions: 'They met together to go and console and comfort him' (v. 11, NRSV). Their motive was not to sort his problems out but to offer comfort and support in his suffering. The first thing they did was also a good idea: 'no one spoke a word to him, for they saw that his suffering was very great' (v. 13, NRSV).

Up to this point they did the right thing. They came with no quick-fix solutions but with a real desire to share with Job and offer support and comfort. When they could think of nothing to say in the presence of such suffering they said nothing, which was also the right thing to do. From this point, however, things went rapidly downhill. In Job 3, Job 'cursed the day of his birth' (v. 1) and went on to lament his circumstances at some length, expressing what was probably a genuine desire that his life would end. So far his friends had simply listened and offered support, but at the start of Job 4 Eliphaz the Temanite asks: 'If one ventures a word with you, will you be offended? But who can keep from speaking?' (v. 2, NRSV). This is the start of a long speech in which Eliphaz argues that Job must have done something for this disaster to come upon him, for instance: 'Think now, who that was innocent ever perished? Or where were the upright cut off?' (v. 7, NRSV).

Most of the rest of the book is the story of the three friends telling Job that there must be a reason for his suffering, and there must be something in his life that merits this treatment by God, while Job keeps denying that this is the case. What is important for our purposes here, however, is simply to observe that it was when Eliphaz decided to speak and claim that there was something that Job had done to create this misfortune that the friends ceased to be a comfort and support and became accusers, actually adding to the woes Job was already experiencing. Significantly at the end of the book it is the three friends who are identified as being at fault. 'The LORD said to Eliphaz the Temanite: "My wrath is kindled against you and against your two friends; for you have not spoken of me what is right, as my servant Job has" ' (42:7, NRSV).

In general terms, the friends people need when they are feeling distressed are those who will accept them for who they are, and be content simply to be with them and listen when they want to speak rather than offering easy solutions. To do this, we must:

- Offer sensible advice when it is asked for.
- Allow the distressed person space to make their own decisions.
- Support them even if we do not agree with everything they are doing.

This does not mean that we passively ignore problems in relationships, attitudes or deliberate disobedience to God's laws. However, the support we do offer should be to encourage the person to do those things that will help their restoration to health, and this needs prayer, gentleness and sensitivity.

In the rest of this section we are going to speak briefly about some practical do's and don'ts – how you can be part of the solution and not part of the problem. Some of these have already been touched on, but are worth repeating.

How to be part of the solution, not part of the problem

Be patient

If you are one of those people who need to see change happen quickly in order to be motivated to continue doing a job, you need to come to terms with the usual nature of depression and anxiety, which can last many weeks or months. If you are someone who quickly becomes impatient it may simply be best to say that this is not your ministry. This can be really hard, of course, if you are in some form of full- or part-time ministry, but the biblical model of the local church as a body is all about different people fulfilling different purposes.

Take mental health issues seriously

Often people with depression and anxiety hardly speak to anyone about their condition. The fact that someone is depressed or anxious may not be immediately obvious, and you may find yourself reacting with surprise if someone you see as outgoing, exuberant and full of life admits to you that they are feeling depressed. In this sort of situation a natural tendency is to play down what is said and make some sort of bland statement that assumes that the difficulty will pass. This is unhelpful because it means that the person has not been really listened to; it is also potentially dangerous because it may well not pass – and may actually worsen without help.

In this regard depression is like many other medical conditions. If properly treated, and if the sufferer is properly supported, it can usually be dealt with very effectively in a reasonable amount of time. Ignored it can lead to very serious consequences, sadly sometimes even death by suicide.

Understand your limitations

Rachel had been under the care of her vicar for a number of months, and appeared to have made significant progress in recovering from depression, when for no apparent reason she began to slip further and further back into depression. Hours of listening and praying for and with Rachel produced no clear benefits – in fact, the downhill slide continued almost unalleviated. The difficulty from the vicar's point of view was that he had really believed that with enough prayer, counselling and ministry she would recover, and that Rachel's faith and his ministry would be the factors used by God to bring healing. Because of this he was unwilling to reach a point where he felt he could say that he had done all he could, and there was a need for more direct medical care from the mental health care profession. He felt a failure, thought he had failed Rachel, and somehow his faith and belief system seemed undermined into the bargain.

Eventually Rachel was admitted to hospital, and looking back on the episode her vicar knew that he should have advised this long before he did. With the benefit of a fuller understanding of psychiatric problems and months of reflection, he also knew that if she had been referred to the appropriate professionals earlier her depression wouldn't have been so severe, and in all probability her recovery would have been more rapid.

When to involve others

This is covered in Chapter 9. Referral to specialist mental health practitioners is often done through the person's own doctor who can advise who best to see, and may occur when:

- The symptoms are worsening and interfering significantly in what they can do.
- They are showing signs of self-neglect, poor self-care or aren't eating and drinking.
- They have suicidal thoughts, cannot see a future and are hopeless. This requires urgent assessment.

Relate positively to mental health care practitioners

It may sound an obvious thing to say, but in the context of helping a patient recover from mental illness church leaders are on the same side as the medical profession. Yet there seems in the minds of some church leaders to be a level of suspicion of the motives and treatments of psychiatrists and psychiatric nurses, and even general practitioners who prescribe antidepressants, that borders on hostility. Sometimes Christians are told not to take medication or counselling that is offered but to trust in God rather than their own doctor, and under no circumstances to allow themselves to be admitted to hospital. This flies in the face of the fact that God has given mankind the gift of intelligence and science so that medicine and research can be carried out. It also ignores the fact that God has called many Christians into the caring professions. In short, such an attitude prevents God from offering help in ways that he would sometimes wish.

This kind of suspicion will often prevent those we care for receiving help that would benefit them. We should also say that suspicion and mistrust can operate in the other direction. A number of doctors, nurses and other health care practitioners regard the ministry of church leaders and pastoral teams as a nuisance. Many who feel this way do so because of the negative effects on patients of some of the more extreme forms of Christian ministry. Having said this, we need to recognise that most of those in mental health care are prepared to welcome and work with clergy, lay leaders and pastoral team members so long as their contribution is positive and constructive.

In our opinion, Christian people who are suffering from depression, anxiety and other mental health problems are usually best helped to recovery by medical personnel and church leaders working together with mutual respect for the experience and skills of the other.

What we have to offer should not be seen as being in competition with the health care professions but complementary to them. So, for instance, pastoral support and prayer is not an alternative to anti-depressants or even hospitalisation, but can be just as much part of the treatment. One example of what we mean here is a Christian hospital in southern England that is staffed by Christian professionals, medical and non-medical, with clergy and lay staff also involved; among other things it cares for people with various forms of mental illness. What is so impressive about its practice is the way that all the staff work together to achieve the same result. After an initial consultation the team that cares for each patient will meet, pray, and plan together a course of treatment and care for each person. In this way the medical, pastoral and support staff work as a unit to achieve the same goals.

Offer unconditional encouragement and support

Most of us would love to be able to 'solve' the difficulties of someone who is depressed or anxious in a few short minutes; to be able to listen, discern what the problem is, pray in faith for healing, and see an instant restoration to full health. Sometimes this happens – our prayer is that it will happen more. Sometimes improvement appears to happen because of the ability of the human mind to believe it has; only later do the symptoms return to show that the healing has been, at best, partial. The reasons why some people are significantly helped, and even healed, through Christian ministry and prayer and others seem to gain little immediate obvious benefit in terms of their condition are, in our opinion, impossible to determine.

Generally, however, we have to be realistic and say that while prayer for healing is fully worthwhile, the healing process often takes much longer than expected, and rapid miracles do not often happen. Recovering from depression or anxiety usually takes a long time – at least weeks, frequently months, and sometimes years.

If we stop to think about it, this is not necessarily a surprise; depression and anxiety are often associated with elements in our life that take time to change, or with difficult aspects of our past. One of the advantages of being a Christian in this situation is that we can believe that God desires, and is able, to help us to live fuller lives. The local church has a significant advantage in its ministry here. Because it only has a limited number of people with mental illness to care for, it should be able to expend quantities of pastoral care and ministry that are simply unavailable to most people.

In the work of Howard Gordon mentioned in Chapter 8, a particularly important factor was the presence of a 'significant other' whose role was essentially to offer support throughout the illness. Of the twenty-three patients interviewed in his research he found that no fewer than seventeen specifically mentioned the role played by a member of the clergy, a close friend, a relative or a spouse. In some cases this support was described as being indispensable. This study demonstrates that simply offering unconditional support and encouragement to someone who is depressed or anxious is extremely worthwhile. When we speak of 'unconditional' encouragement and support we do not mean that there should be no time or access limits within the relationship. In fact, it is important to establish some kind of framework within which our support and encouragement is offered. Rather we mean that we agree to keep offering this support whatever direction the illness takes. Likewise, if the person makes choices that we consider unwise and are likely to cause further difficulty, then we don't withdraw our support. If we are on the receiving end of anger and frustration simply because we are there and within striking distance, we should not walk out on the relationship because our feelings have been hurt, but instead maintain our involvement for as long as it is needed.

Pay attention to those in leadership roles

An additional problem for someone with depression and anxiety may be their church commitments. Indeed church leaders, ordained or lay, are not immune from developing depression and anxiety. Within churches there can be an incredible amount of work to do. Individuals may find themselves taking on more tasks even when they are struggling to carry out their usual church 'duties'. Leaders of Bible study or fellowship groups may have difficulty leading and interacting with people; leaders of prayer groups may have difficulty praying; individuals may be worried about their ability to teach or lead worship. When someone is depressed and anxious it may be very difficult for them to say that they cannot manage, and if they do they may be concerned that this will lead to criticism and judgment by the leadership team and other church members.

Therefore if you are aware of an individual suffering from depression and anxiety, consider the tasks they have within the church. Discuss the role the individual wishes to play within the life of the church during the time of their illness. It may be appropriate to suggest that they discontinue some of their church-related activities for a while. Make it clear that there is no pressure to resume this work within a set period of time and that you will find others to take on their responsibilities for the time being. Do not leave it to the individual suffering from depression and anxiety to find others to do their tasks. Discuss what the individual wants you to tell others. Having done all of this, remember to discuss this with the individual again at a suitable time. Hopefully there will come a time when the individual feels well enough to resume some of their church activities. Discuss ways in which this can be done gradually. Do not assume that the individual will launch into everything right away. As they start becoming involved again, remember to check out how they are getting on.

SPECIFIC DIFFICULTIES AND DANGEROUS PITFALLS

A number of difficulties can occur when people with mental health problems attend churches. Whether the person is a Christian or not, sometimes difficulties can arise that raise issues of how best to respond in ways that balance our loving responsibilities to the individual and to the wider church membership.

A disruptive influence

Sometimes a person's distressed state, particularly if they are very unwell, will result in inappropriate and disruptive behaviour. This can involve verbal interruptions, physically moving around at inappropriate times, and other behaviour that has the effect of disrupting services, meetings, house groups and so on.

How you respond to this sort of behaviour will depend a great deal on the sort of church you belong to and the kind of meeting that is involved. Some fellowships will have a far more relaxed style than others and will hardly notice someone wandering round the church. Others will be quieter and more formal and will not be able to tolerate much disruptive behaviour at all. A good policy in general terms is to leave the person alone unless and until the point is reached where the level of disruption is affecting others and whatever is happening is being disrupted. There should be someone whose job it is, when this point is reached, to intervene gently, and take the person to a seat or, if necessary, outside the building. It will usually be possible to help the disturbed person calm down and behave more moderately, particularly if they are sitting next to someone whose role is to look after them during the meeting.

Someone who has become very dependent or in need of excessive reassurance

One of the most common problems in churches where there is ministry to people with mental illness is that of dependency where the person over-invests in a particular relationship, especially with a church leader. A state of dependency has generally been reached when the person receiving some form of ministry is unable to function properly for any length of time without some form of contact with the person who is offering ministry. Signs of this include receiving telephone calls at all times of day and night, spending frequent and excessive amounts of time in the company of the helper, and an inability to make decisions of any consequence without reference to the person or persons on whom they have become dependent.

Unlike most professional situations it is very difficult to walk away from someone asking for help in a church setting, when home addresses and telephone numbers are well known. It is difficult to say 'No' to someone asking for help when we share the same church fellowship, and so the creation of dependency is a rather common experience in church life.

When faced with this situation:

- In the long term, dependency is unhealthy for both the helper and the person who is receiving the help. Some problems may be dealt with, and some relief given, but in general terms what tends to happen is that issues are covered up rather than being dealt with, and both parties become too close to the situation to see things objectively.
- Some sort of framework is essential in ministering to people who are distressed. Some sort of contract, albeit a verbal one, should be drawn up that specifies frequency and time of contact, and apart from genuine emergencies this should be enforced, however difficult that may seem at first.
- If you find that you are in a situation where someone is dependent upon you in this way it is important for their sake as well as your own that the dependency comes to an end. Our suggestion is that you speak to another church leader, perhaps a senior figure, and share together how it might be possible for you to withdraw from the relationship or manage it differently, perhaps by sharing the support.
- Training in listening skills and learning how to establish a

framework for help would be a good thing for most churches to undertake. A number of Christian organisations exist with appropriate experience in this area. We suggest that you use one that approaches the matter from a counselling perspective and has properly accredited counsellors on its staff. They may also be able to offer specific supervision and support when difficulties arise.

Hygiene issues

Sometimes people with mental health problems such as schizophrenia or dementia may put on excessive weight, develop poor personal hygiene (e.g. be very smelly or dishevelled and have unwashed hair for weeks on end) and not be aware of the impact on others of this. This can cause difficulties for those who sit nearby in services and raises the question of how best to respond. Such problems are likely to be a part of their mental health problem, and need to be seen as such. It is important that they feel accepted, but of course people who do not know about their condition may find the poor hygiene a real problem.

A practical suggestion is for someone who already has a relationship with this person and is functioning in a supportive role already to speak gently and carefully to the person concerned. It may well be possible to liaise with someone like the community psychiatric nurse assigned to this patient – they may have one – and try to work together on a strategy for care, including matters of personal hygiene. Nevertheless, in the last analysis it would be a terrible condemnation of any church if someone in this situation felt unwanted, and that should be safeguarded against at all costs. A positive way of seeing such difficulties is that it shows that the church is reaching out to people with problems – as it should.

PASTORAL TEAMS – THE NEED FOR A CLEAR STRUCTURE AND ROLE

We have chosen the term 'pastoral team' rather than 'counselling team' because of the importance of recognising that counselling is a highly skilled profession requiring years of training and a long apprenticeship. While some pastoral work may have counselling elements, particularly if there has been some level of appropriate training, the distinction is a very important one.

One practical step almost every church of any size can take is to establish a pastoral team. Each church should be able to identify those who have gifts of encouragement, support and pastoral care. If it is a small church, it may be that such support is best offered by just one or two people, or links could be made with other churches to provide a joint local resource. In others, a larger pastoral support team could develop.

There are some key qualities that are vital for membership of such a team, and people without clear evidence of these qualities should probably be discouraged from joining.

- Empathy – defined as the ability to get alongside and put oneself in the place of the person.
- Warmth – being able to show human caring, interest and support to others.
- Acceptance – willingness to work from where someone is, accepting them as they are.
- Genuineness – being yourself – listening and relating to the person honestly and naturally. Not claiming to know or provide all the answers.
- Patience – the ability to keep going, if necessary at a slow pace, over a long period of time.

Read some of the interactions that Jesus had with others to see just how well he achieved this in his own ministry.

It could well be that the paid or voluntary leadership of a church are not the best people either to lead or work on such a team, even if they need to offer oversight in a general sense. Wisdom and humility are needed to discern who can best serve such needs within each individual church setting. If such a team is established it is important for it to be properly resourced; to have a budget, team times where people can minister to one another, and a programme of training in listening, counselling and prayer ministry skills.

Practical issues about pastoral teams

Visibility

How can you make sure the team is visible and easily contacted as part of a formal pastoral team? Practical issues such as who these people are, how to contact them, what is on offer if they are contacted, etc. should be made widely available. Boards with photographs, names, telephone numbers, etc. can help, but the best way is if such people are also visible within the church and their role is discussed intermittently in the services. This may be formalised; for example, with the chance to meet the team for discussion or prayer after the end of certain services each month.

Clear leadership/accountability

A clear system of leadership and accountability is required. Sometimes pastoral teams are allowed to work with little discussion of their role and practice by the church leadership. A written policy of accountability and membership of the team should also be created. A named person should be in charge and responsible for any team that is created. No pastoral team should be left unsupervised by the wider church leadership. A mental health professional in the church or who works locally could be asked to join an advisory panel, which should also have input from the church leaders.

Select and regularly review the membership of the team

People who have experienced mental health problems themselves often seek to offer help to others. This in itself is not a problem, but where motivations to help others are excessively mixed with meeting their own personal needs, difficulties may arise. Wisdom is required here by the team and by the church leaders.

Offer effective training

A key to offering help is 'above all, do no harm'. To achieve this, people working in this role need to have both effective skills in relating to people, and also specific skills in counselling or psychotherapy that often require extensive training. The most important skill to learn first of all is generally how to listen. There are organisations with trained counsellors who are willing to teach listening skills to church pastoral teams from a specifically Christian perspective, and we recommend this approach.

Training should address:

- What to do when someone expresses suicidal ideas. Such people need to make *urgent* contact with their doctor.
- What to do when someone is behaving oddly in a way that suggests that a major mental disorder such as schizophrenia is present. Such people need to make contact with their doctor.
- Confidentiality – keeping private those things that are discussed in trust.

To do this well, a specific budget for training is required and this should be reviewed on an annual basis.

Potential dangers in pastoral teams

Unfortunately, although sometimes pastoral teams can be helpful, various pitfalls also exist.

A misuse of power

Working in pastoral teams provides the potential for the abuse of power. People who are distressed, depressed or anxious often find that their confidence and personal resources are at a low level. This may leave them open to manipulation or abuse by others. This may include:

- emotional abuse.
- physical abuse including violence.
- sexual abuse such as inappropriate massage, hugging or sexual contact by the person supposedly offering them help. This is discussed in more detail shortly.
- spiritual abuse with unmerited requests to repent, confess sins, etc. when the motive is to reinforce the ego of the team member, not to re-establish the health of the sufferer.

Betrayed confidentiality

Pastoral team members are in a privileged position of trust. Unfortunately this trust can be betrayed. We have all probably heard someone at prayer meetings say that they are supporting Person X who really needs prayer at the moment, because of . . . Unfortunately, sometimes the motive here is not for X, but rather for the helper to look good either to themselves or to others in the church.

The dangers of inappropriate sexual relationships

Sometimes people with mental illness may be sexually disinhibited, and individuals in a so-called caring role may take advantage of those who are vulnerable as a result of their illness. Those offering help to people who are distressed, whether part of a team or when working as an individual, should be aware of this. Clear rules on how they relate to those they wish to help are required. There is a strong argument that having two people routinely present is best practice for support sessions if there is any possibility of actual or alleged sexual misconduct. This is especially the case when the counselling is with someone of a different sex, when a younger person is being counselled, and always when discussions of an intimate sexual nature occur, which requires two (preferably of the same sex) team members present. This helps the person who is talking about their problems, and also provides a valuable protection for the church workers themselves.

Practical suggestion: create a mental health care policy
Write out a 'mental health care policy' for your church, or perhaps a charter for people suffering from depression or anxiety. Try to say what those who are mentally ill should be able to expect from your church, and what you can realistically offer. Perhaps you could present this to the church leadership and even encourage the church to adopt it. Be realistic as you do this; try to be honest about what resources you really have available and what is actually achievable.

HEALING AND DELIVERANCE

You may have had the same experience as this minister:

> As the minister of a local church I had never before encountered someone who heard voices in their head, and once I knew those voices were telling the person to harm herself, all my theological instincts told me that these voices must be coming from demonic forces possessing the young woman I was praying for. Whether or not this was true is still something of a mystery, but the real eye-opener came a few months later when I began speaking to a number of people in an acute psychiatric ward, and came to the realisation that such voices were actually quite a common occurrence, and a 'normal' part of a number of mental health problems.

This illustrates a difficulty in the area of pastoral care for the mentally ill; so much of the ministry that occurs springs out of a lack of knowledge of the nature and course of conditions such as depression and anxiety – in particular many church leaders have little idea just how common some of these difficulties are. Our suggestion is that before addressing issues such as healing and deliverance anyone seeking to offer prayer ministry and significant pastoral support would benefit greatly from first learning about the conditions they are ministering to.

Healing and deliverance are separate but strongly related matters; they are also issues that arouse strong feelings and responses from most sections of the Christian Church, and beyond it. The treatment that is required to deal with this subject would fill at least one book, and lies outside the scope and, indeed, the principal purpose of this book, which is essentially a self-help book for sufferers. Nevertheless, rather than completely avoid the issues we want to suggest some guidelines and refer those interested to one or two further sources of help.

Healing: general principles

We are all called to pray for difficult situations, and for Christians it is a natural response to pray for healing and peace. Prayer for healing presents most church leaders with something of a dilemma. In the New Testament faith was always required for healing to take place; as often as not it is the faith of the person praying that is important, but also frequently faith on the part of the recipient. On the other hand, the practical experience of most church leaders is that a high percentage of those prayed for are not instantly supernaturally healed. Knowing this, how do we pray with faith? Our belief is that confidence in the power of God needs to be balanced by our knowledge that many will not be healed in a direct, immediate sense.

Here are some guidelines for prayer:

- Do pray for healing, whether this is instant healing or natural healing over time with or without medical help. In addition, pray for peace and help while we wait is important.
- Do not raise unrealistic expectations; in particular avoid claiming that healing has taken place when there is little evidence to suggest it has.

- Never burden the recipient of prayer with accusations of failure. For instance, never suggest that healing hasn't taken place because of the person's sin or lack of faith.
- Whatever the outcome of the prayer for healing, ensure that there is appropriate pastoral support for the person being prayed for.
- Ensure that those praying for healing are accountable to the church leadership as a whole.

Deliverance: general principles

We believe that trying a deliverance route when the problem is mental illness not only will not help, but makes matters worse by introducing or reinforcing in the individual's mind the existence/influence of an evil spirit.

- The Bible confirms the existence of demonic powers.
- Mental illness is not caused directly by such powers.
- On the rare occasions when demonic forces cause mental distress there will be characteristics of the presentation that make it distinct from cases of mental illness; in particular there are likely to be occult elements involved and the usual pattern of symptoms seen within mental disorders will be absent.
- Deliverance should be considered only when a mental illness has been excluded or effectively treated, and when the church leadership and pastoral teams think it is necessary. So first ensure that the patient has told their doctor of all their symptoms.
- If demonic influence is suspected, try to involve people such as those mentioned opposite who have experience in this kind of spiritual warfare. Local churches may find that they have members who have gifts of spiritual discernment; however, these should be formally tested and recognised within the church and not merely be based upon the opinion of the person themself. Some denominations and church groups have specified regional advisers who have particular experience in this area. This should not, however, bypass the existing church leadership.

- Deliverance ministry should never be undertaken by one person acting alone (Matthew 18:19–20).
- Ensure that there is accountability to the church leadership as a whole for those undertaking a deliverance ministry.
- Ensure that strong pastoral support is available before any deliverance ministry takes place for the person and for those praying for them.

Where to go for further support

There is an informal network of centres of healing in the UK, and for further help we suggest contacting the following:

Burrswood, Groombridge, Tunbridge Wells, Kent TN3 9PY.
Tel: 01892-863637
Web-site: www.burrswood.org.uk

The Acorn Christian Foundation, Whitehill Chase, High St, Bordon, Hants GU35 0AP.
Tel: 01420-478121
Web-site: www.acornchristian.org

Summary

The following summarises some of the key actions that may be helpful in supporting those who are distressed in your church.

- Work towards a culture within your own church that 'allows' Christians to be distressed. Encourage an atmosphere of love, support, openness and honesty when such needs arise.
- Sermons, house groups and other teachings should intermittently cover topics like depression, anxiety, bereavement and distress. This allows such topics to be seen as a normal part of life for many Christians. These teachings provide an opportunity to discuss how faith can help support those who are distressed. Examples for discussion include the experience of Job as discussed above.

- Stick to the basics – let the person know that they are accepted and loved by God. Don't get into repetitive arguments about God's love for them – a simple statement will suffice. Show love through your own attitude.
- Listen and ask questions to help you to understand how the person with mental health problems feels. Don't try to immediately solve their problems for them. Asking questions may be more helpful than 'telling' the person your own answers.
- Provide 'permission' so that the person can relinquish certain tasks in church/not lead groups, etc. if they have such a workload and this is proving part of the problem. Similar advice is also relevant for other areas of life such as some home and work commitments.
- Protect the person. Watch out for and try to correct unhelpful relationships with others in the church (such as the person surrounding themselves with others who also feel distressed).
- Decide who are the best people to help in the church. People with a calling and gifts in the area of pastoral care and encouragement should be identified. Create a pastoral support team that is well trained and staffed by people who are in it for the right reasons – to support others rather than to meet their own inner needs. In any church, God will have provided people with the gifts and calling to support this work. Try to identify and support these people in this work, and make sure that this is offered within a clear structure that is monitored to ensure that something that is safe, effective and helpful is offered.

CLOSING PRAYER

When you can, pray this prayer silently or preferably aloud.

Father God,
I reflect on the pages that I have just read. I think of people I know and care for who are in distress at this present time. I think of my

local church/fellowship and consider how it deals with those distressed, depressed and anxious.

Forgive me for the times when I have got it wrong – not saying or doing the right thing, not understanding or assuming that I had the right answer. Give me more understanding of depression and anxiety and grant me greater patience and wisdom to deal more effectively with those who suffer. Give me the wisdom to know how to tackle specific problems.

Help me to lead and teach others to have greater understanding and patience as well. Guide me as I lead the church in its ministry of caring and healing.

I thank you for all those involved in the caring professions, for those treating the people I know to be unwell. I pray that we may be able to work in partnership, giving each other mutual respect. Help us to put any differences aside.

Thank you for the Christian hospital where physical, spiritual and psychological treatments are all offered together. Thank you that this exciting development has occurred. I pray that this will lead to great benefits for those who attend, and that it may provide a useful model for other such projects.

I pray for other church leaders reading this chapter. Give us wisdom and guidance to know the ways in which you are asking us to move forward in our ministry to those suffering from mental health problems.

Amen.

REFERENCES

Forbes, C. (1983), *The Religion of Power*, Marc Europe: Bromley.

Gray, A. (1994), *An Introduction to the Therapeutic Frame*, Routledge Press.

Appendix 1

Hints and tips for overcoming common symptoms in depression and anxiety

Lifestyle changes

Making changes in your day-to-day life may help to improve your mood. It is important to take care of yourself and be kind to yourself. This may be difficult if you have been living a busy and hectic life. The following is a short practical summary of some helpful lifestyle changes that you can make to help improve common symptoms of anxiety and depression.

Symptoms	Hints and tips
A decreased appetite	1. Eating a balanced range of foods is important to keep both your physical and mental strength up. 2. Try to eat foods that contain energy such as protein, fats and carbohydrate, and also fruit and vegetables.
An increased appetite	1. Try to eat a balanced and sensible diet. 2. Plan your shopping to avoid impulse buys, particularly of carbohydrates such as biscuits or chocolate.

	3. In particular, try to avoid any increase in alcohol intake. It will add to your depression or anxiety. 4. Try to eat meals while sitting at a meal table. Avoid snacks or bringing extra food to the table. If you want to eat more, force yourself to get up so that it is a conscious decision to eat it.
Increased weight	Reduced activity levels and increased appetite may cause weight gain. Think about: 1. Introducing some mild exercise into your day (this may also boost your mood). Start with a short 5–10 minute walk. 2. Eating a balanced diet: vegetables and fruit will also prevent constipation. 3. Eat little but often.
Decreased weight	1. Eating a balanced range of foods is important to keep both your physical and mental strength up. 2. This should include foods that contain energy such as protein, fats and carbohydrate, and also fruit and vegetables. Make sure you are also drinking a normal volume of fluids such as water so that you don't become dehydrated.
Reduced energy	1. Low energy is a common problem in depression and anxiety. A vicious circle can arise. By reducing your activity, your muscles are used less. This causes them to weaken and they will feel painful and tired when they are used again. 2. An effective way of overcoming this is to plan a graded increase in your activity in a step-by-step way. This often leads to a boost in how you feel mentally as well as physically. 3. Remember, don't overdo exercise. Plan a slow increase in what you do. Just five minutes of exercise (e.g. walking up and downstairs three times a day to begin with) is the sort of level to aim at if you have not been doing any recent exercise. Slowly increase it over the next few days and weeks. 4. *If you have a physical illness, please discuss this with*

	your doctor and agree a plan for this graded increase in activity. 5. A common symptom in depression is to feel worse first thing in the morning. If you notice this, plan to do activities (such as going out) later on in the day. 6. Finally, don't throw yourself into this too quickly. Do it one step at a time.
A reduced sex drive	1. A reduced sex drive is common in depression. If you have a spouse try to discuss this with them. 2. Your sex drive will improve (as will other symptoms) towards its previous levels as you recover from the anxiety or depression. 3. In men, antidepressants can sometimes cause problems with having erections or ejaculating. If this is a difficulty for you, discuss this with your doctor. 4. If you find it difficult talking about this with your spouse please do try to discuss it with your health care practitioner.
Symptoms of constipation	Constipation commonly occurs in depression and can be a side effect of some antidepressants. Simple changes can help: • Eat vegetables, fruit, bran and fibre. • Exercise helps constipation. • Drink a reasonable amount of fluids.
Symptoms of pain	1. Pain such as chest pain, stomach pain and headaches may be worsened by depression and anxiety. If this is the case, treating the mental health problem is the best approach. 2. If the pain is linked to the depression or anxiety, you may find that painkillers such as aspirin and paracetamol do not seem to be very effective. 3. If this is the case, it is important to avoid building up the dose of painkillers you are taking. This may cause new physical symptoms and for some painkillers may even cause more symptoms of pain and possibly addiction.

	4. In this case, treatment with antidepressants is often more effective. Please discuss this with your doctor.
Symptoms of physical agitation	1. Focusing your attention on these symptoms can sometimes worsen physical agitation. This mental tension then adds to the unpleasant feelings of physical tension. 2. If the agitation feelings are very distressing, consider using medication to reduce it. Many effective short-term medications (which are not addictive) are available. Antidepressant medication will often improve symptoms of agitation caused by anxiety or depression. Discuss this with your doctor.

Understanding sleep problems

Sleeping problems are common and affect large numbers of people. At times, sleep can be disrupted for a variety of different reasons.

What is sleep?

In spite of the fact that we spend around a third of our lives asleep, it is something that we often take for granted until we are unable to do it. The amount of sleep each individual needs varies throughout their life. Babies and young children need a lot more sleep than older adults. Many people find that by the time they reach their sixties or seventies, the amount of sleep they need has dropped by up to several hours a day. The average time we sleep is often said to be about eight hours but this is only true for some people. There is a wide, normal, healthy sleep range. Some people sleep only four to six hours a day whereas others can sleep for as many as ten or twelve hours a day. Both extremes are quite normal.

Factors affecting sleep

Think about your sleeping environment

Make sure your bed and mattress are comfortable and that your bedroom isn't too hot or cold. Are there any bright lights coming in through your curtains, or intermittent loud noises that wake you up? Think about fitting curtain linings to keep light out and double glazing to keep heat in and noise out. Wear ear plugs if necessary to block out noise – available from pharmacies/chemists.

The following may hinder you sleeping well, so try to avoid

- Stimulants – avoid drinking too much coffee, tea, hot chocolate or soft drinks that contain caffeine – around five cups or glasses a day is the maximum you should drink. Switch to decaffeinated drinks if you drink more than this. You will find more about this at the end of the Appendix.
- Watch your alcohol intake. Alcohol causes sleep to be shallow and unrefreshing.
- Stimulating exercise just before bed can cause you to become more alert and this may prevent you from falling off to sleep.
- If possible do some exercise during the day – fitter people enjoy a better quality of sleep.

Establish a set routine for sleep

- Try to get into a routine. Go to bed and get up at a regular time. Set your alarm clock to wake you up and then get up at the same time each day – avoid lying in bed each morning.
- Avoid taking naps during the day. It upsets your body clock.

Have a wind-down time leading up to going to bed

- Try to wind down during the second half of the evening. Don't work right up to bedtime.
- Get into a relaxing routine leading up to bedtime – have a hot drink (non-caffeinated), a bath, read or listen to soft music or worship music.
- You may feel tense and anxious as bedtime approaches. Techniques that help you relax will help the onset of sleep. Practise a relaxation routine that suits you.
- Only go to bed when you are sleepy tired.

When in bed

- Don't try too hard to fall asleep – this can keep you awake!
- If you can't sleep after ten to twenty minutes, just get up, go to another room and then return to bed only when you feel sleepy tired again.
- If you find yourself waking up repeatedly during the night, get up and do something else (e.g. read, watch television, but avoid scary films that may wake you up still further) until you feel sleepy tired, then go to bed again. *It is important not to lie in or to sleep or take a nap during the next day* even if you feel tired because this will upset your body clock and add to your problems.
- Avoid watching television or working in bed.
- If you have an illuminated alarm clock, turn it away from you so you don't 'clock watch' throughout the night.
- Keep a sleep diary; each day record your sleep experiences and your daily activities to discuss with your doctor.

Dealing with intrusive thoughts when you are in bed

Thoughts about daytime events and problems are often suppressed until bedtime. This may be your first opportunity to think about them and make plans. The time to think things through is before you go to bed. If you find these sorts of thoughts popping into your mind, be determined to switch your mind off when you go to bed. Leave fleeting thoughts alone. Note the thoughts down on a piece of paper, put them aside for later. You can choose to look at them again tomorrow when you are awake and have time to think them through.

The role of caffeine in sleeplessness

Caffeine is a mild stimulant that makes you feel alert and awake. It can be found in coffee, tea, cola, cocoa and some other soft drinks. Too much caffeine can be a problem because in higher doses it can cause a number of unwanted side effects such as:

- Anxiety and panic symptoms.
- Sleep disturbances.
- Headaches and shakiness.
- Restlessness and irritability.
- Feelings of sickness and stomach complaints.
- Palpitations and irregular heart beats.

Caffeine is physically addictive and if you drink many cups of coffee each day for a few months you will quickly find that you need to drink a greater amount to have the same effect. If you are drinking more than four to five glasses/cups of caffeinated drinks, you should consider reducing the amount you drink. Do this gradually. If you stop suddenly, you may suffer withdrawal symptoms that include: throbbing headache, nausea, lethargy and irritability.

In order to reduce your caffeine intake, start by drinking weaker tea or coffee, try decaffeinated drinks or drink caffeine-free drinks such as herbal teas, water or fruit juices.

Premenstrual syndrome (PMS), depression and anxiety

For some women, the symptoms of depression and anxiety may be worse around their periods or may only occur at this time. In addition to working through this book, the following may be useful:

Diet

Don't go on a diet but change your eating pattern:

- Drink more water.
- Eat more green vegetables and salad.
- Eat more fruit and nuts.
- Eat more pasta, rice, chicken and fish.
- Reduce foods with lots of sugar and salt.
- Reduce caffeinated drinks.
- Reduce the intake of 'junk foods'.
- Reduce smoking and alcohol intake.

Exercise

This will help to relieve tension and give a sense of wellbeing. Start exercising slowly and gradually increase it.

Medication

- Some women find vitamin B complex and oil of evening primrose useful. If you want to try this, check with your doctor first.
- Your doctor may prescribe the oral contraceptive pill. This should reduce the symptoms of PMS.
- Antidepressants may be helpful, in particular the group called SSRIs (selective serotonin reuptake inhibitors).

Thought Investigation Worksheet: Identifying my extreme and unhelpful thinking

1. Situation/ relationship or practical problem when your mood unhelpfully altered	2. Altered emotional and physical feelings	3. What immediate thoughts are present at the time?
Think in detail: Where am I, what am I doing? Consider: • The time: What time of day is it? • The place: Where am I? • The people: Who is present? Who am I with? • The events: What has been said/What events happened?	Am I: • Low or sad? Guilty? • Worried, tense, anxious or panicky? • Angry or irritable? • Ashamed? a. State the feelings clearly. Try to be as precise as possible. If more than one feeling occurs, underline the most powerful feeling. b. How powerful is this feeling? (0-100%) c. Note down any strong physical sensations you notice.	What is going through my mind? How do I see: • Myself, my relationship with God, how others see me? • The current events/situation? • What might happen in the future? • My own body, behaviour or performance? • Any memories/images? a. State the thought(s) clearly. Try to be as precise as possible. If more than one thought occurs, underline the most powerful thought. b. Rate how strongly you believe the most powerful thought at the time (0–100%)
My situation:	**a. My feelings:** **b. Powerfulness:** **c. Physical sensations:**	**a. My immediate thoughts:** **b. Rating of belief in the most powerful thought at the time:** 0% 100% |--------------------------------|

4. What unhelpful thinking style(s) occur?	5. Impact of the immediate thought(s)
1. Bias against myself. 2. Putting a negative slant on things (Negative mental filter). 3. Having a gloomy view of the future/jumping to the worst conclusion/catastrophic thinking. 4 Negative views about how others see me (Mind-reading). 5. Bearing all responsibility. 6. Making extreme statements/rules e.g. using 'must', 'should', 'ought', 'always', 'got to', 'typical' and 'never' statements. If any of the styles are present, you have identified an *extreme* thought.	a. What did I do differently? Consider any: • Reduced activity. • Unhelpful behaviours. b. What was the impact on: • Myself? • My relationship with God? • My view of others? • How I felt? • What I said? • What I did? • Overall, was the impact helpful or unhelpful? If there is an unhelpful impact, you have identified an *unhelpful* thought.
Thinking styles present: No(s):	**a. What I did differently:** **b. Overall, is it helpful or unhelpful for me to believe the thought?** Helpful ☐ Unhelpful ☐

Thought Challenge Worksheet: Challenging my extreme and unhelpful thought

6. Reasons supporting the immediate thought	7. Reasons against the immediate thought
List all the reasons why I believed the immediate thought at the time.	Answer the following questions: • What would Jesus/God say to me about how he sees this thought? How would he encourage me? • Are there any other ways of explaining the situation that are more accurate? Is there anything to make me think the thought is incorrect? • If I wasn't feeling anxious/depressed, what would I say? • What would I tell a Christian friend who said the same thing? • What helpful things would other people say to me about it? • Have I heard *different opinions* from others about the thought?
My evidence supporting the immediate thought:	**My evidence against the immediate thought:**

8. Come to a balanced conclusion	9. My plan for putting the balanced conclusion into practice
Use the answers from Columns 6 and 7 to try to come up with a *balanced, truthful* and *helpful* conclusion. Look for a *balanced conclusion* that you can believe. This should be based on *all* the information you have available to you and bear in mind the reasons for and against believing the immediate thought.	• How can I change what I do to reinforce my balanced conclusion? • How can I undermine my immediate negative thought by acting against it?
My balanced conclusion: **a. Rating of my belief in the balanced conclusion:** 0% 100% |--------------------------------| **b. Re-rating of my belief in the immediate thought:** 0% 100% |--------------------------------|	**My plan to put the balanced conclusion into practice:**